TOUR de KENT

The day the world's biggest bike race came to the Garden of England

TOUR de KENT

The day the world's biggest bike race came to the Garden of England

Fred Atkins

breedon **books**
PUBLISHING

First published in Great Britain in 2009 by
The Breedon Books Publishing Company Limited
Breedon House, 3 The Parker Centre,
Derby, DE21 4SZ.

ISBN 978-1-85983-738-2
Printed and bound by MKT Print, Slovenia

CONTENTS

Would you like one of the images in this book?

To order any of the Kent Messenger pictures used in this book, visit
www.kentonline.co.uk
You can also order pictures at the reception desks in any of our offices or by
telephone, on 01622 794670.

Dedication

For Wendy and Sylvia.

PROLOGUE

On 8 July 2007 Martyn Peal, a cycling fanatic from Wateringbury, was waiting for the Tour de France to arrive at Crittenden Road in Capel, a hill that had slipped under the radar of the organisers of the world's biggest bike race, but one known to local cyclists for providing a short, sharp shock. Peal had already watched the race pass through his home village around an hour earlier. He then jumped in his car, bombed down the East Peckham bypass and picked his spot at the roadside, knowing this relatively unknown incline would provide one of the best views of the action in the whole 120-mile route.

Crowds were 20 people deep in certain sections through the major population centres, but Crittenden Road attracted only a smattering of fans, mainly canny locals and tourists who got lucky.

Having secured himself the best seat in the house, there was one thing Peal was determined not to do.

'You know when you're watching cycling on the telly and you see people running alongside the riders? And you're thinking "they're idiots…"'

He had a point. Mountain stages of bike races are notorious for over-enthusiastic fans, who run alongside the riders, screaming either encouragement or abuse, usually (though not exclusively) with a Basque flag tied around their necks.

At a football match police and stewards can head off pitch invasions, but during a bike race it is a logistical impossibility to prevent streakers from grabbing a share of the athletes' limelight.

The fan watching on television longs to see the streaker 'clotheslined', to borrow a rugby term, and on rare occasions riders have reacted to the provocation – one of the most memorable reactions came when the Italian Gianni Bugno thrust his front wheel into the nose of a spectator who had knocked him off his bike.

Yet when Peal caught sight of David Millar and four other breakaway riders clambering up Crittenden Road, or Capel Hill as it is also known, a switch flicked inside his head.

And he began to run.

'I couldn't help it,' he later admitted. 'I just started running alongside him, shouting "Come on David!" and as soon as I'd stopped, someone else started.'

This is the effect that watching the Tour de France can have on the initiated. Even the non-fanatical can be trapped in its tractor beam.

An estimated two million people watched the Tour pass through South London and Kent on 8 July, 25 times the crowd for a sell-out Cup Final at Wembley and 100 times the crowd for a Lord's test match.

In this context, the prevailing wisdom of the media that cycling is somehow a minority sport is rendered absurd. This was an event that captured the imagination of whole sections of the population who normally have no interest in sport, and as such the day represented the greatest mobilisation of the public ever seen in peacetime Kent. And for that reason, 8 July deserves a proper historical record.

This book will tell the story of that extraordinary day, the two million people who witnessed it and the riders who provided a compelling narrative throughout the stage. It does not shy away from the drug scandals that hit the race once it had left Kent. Writing about the Tour without mentioning drugs would be like writing about George Best and leaving out the alcohol. But it is not a book for people who want blow-by-blow accounts of negotiations that took place in anonymous local government offices prior to the racing, nor does it cater for the kind of reader who likes to be outraged by tales of frivolous spending by local authorities.

Anyone who objects to the idea that Kent County Council should have spent £1 million to bring the race to the county should look elsewhere (I recommend *The Daily Mail*).

However, if you are looking for a memento of one of the most remarkable days in this county's history, hopefully this book will do 8 July 2007 justice.

Chapter 1

TOUR de... KENT?

The original idea was born of nothing more altruistic than a desire to sell newspapers. First staged in 1903, the Tour de France was conceived as a promotional vehicle for the sports paper *L'Auto*, the logic being that if millions of people would turn up at the roadside to watch a bicycle race, they would then want to read about what they had seen in a newspaper.

Over the course of a century the Tour evolved into a three-week, multi-stage race, with around 200 riders competing to be the first to complete a 2,000-mile circuit of France. From its inception, the Tour captivated the French public and, when the race made one of its periodic border crossings many years later, France's neighbours were equally entranced.

Yet the success of the Kent stage in 2007 was anything but inevitable. Kent is not a county that has the sporting heritage of Tyneside, Merseyside or Greater Manchester. Even compared to more traditional 'shires' like Leicestershire, Notts and Northants (and acknowledging the glorious exception to the rule provided by Kelly Holmes) it is an underachieving county. Its main gift to the world of sport is the game of cricket, believed to have first been played in its modern format in and around the Weald sometime during the 17th century. The game can now boast tens of millions of world-wide devotees, but in Kent itself it is, in terms of both participation and spectators, a minority sport. Attendances for county matches, though healthy by national standards, are poor, with perhaps 2,000 attending a County Championship game on a good day and 6,000 turning out for higher-profile one-day fixtures.

The county's only Football League club, Gillingham, have never risen higher than the middle reaches of the second flight of the English League system, a level they only played at between the years of 2000 and 2005. Though they managed to pull 30,000 fairweather supporters to Play-off Finals at Wembley in 1999 and 2000, Gillingham, now in the fourth tier of English football, average barely 5,000 fans for home games at their Priestfield stadium. Depressingly, Charlton Athletic, a South London club, claim to attract a greater number of supporters from Kent to the Valley.

Attendances at non-League football games (some Kent League clubs struggle to pull in 50 paying customers) are often lower than those in the county's sports bars when Premier League games or England internationals are shown.

The top sporting venue in the county is the Brands Hatch motor-racing circuit, which can accommodate six-figure crowds and used to host the British Grand Prix until it was superseded by Silverstone in the 1980s. Although Brands continues to thrive, despite the lack of Formula 1 action, for every one of the 100,000 people who watched the 2007 British Superbikes event at the West Kingsdown circuit, 20 people watched the Tour de France when it came to Kent.

It was not immediately apparent why.

To quote Dick Pound, former head of WADA, the worldwide anti-doping agency, when the Tour de France came to town in 2007, cycling's image was 'in the toilet'. Critics argued it had about as much credibility as wrestling, and not without justification. A percentage of riders were ingesting drugs in quantities even deformed, greased-up body-builders would baulk at. Champion after champion was exposed as a fraud. Days

The happy couple: Jean Marie Leblanc and Ken Livingstone at the QEII centre in London, where the route for the 2007 Tour was unveiled.

Photograph courtesy KM Group

"Bonjour...je m'appelle Ken Livingstone."

before the start of the race the author and ITV reporter Matt Rendell, who ought to have had a vested interest in the event's success, told me he thought the last untainted winner of the Tour de France was Greg LeMond, who had been victorious 17 years previously, and even then he added that the musculature of the average cyclist had 'evolved' by 1989.

Locally there were no scandals to report on, but the sport's overall scene was pretty desolate. In the regional Press, cycling would get a nib, or in a good week a sidebar, until the arrival of Ashford's Jamie Staff on the BMX and track-racing scene belatedly bucked the trend – not that any potential track star could train anywhere near Ashford: the nearest velodrome was and remains London's Herne Hill.

Nor was cycling a popular participant sport in 2007, as opposed to a leisure activity. A few 'testers' competed in time-trials, ploughing up and down the A20 or A21 for 10 or 25 miles at a time, dodging the juggernauts and assorted other motorised lunatics to try and beat their personal bests. An even smaller number belonged to the Kent League, which offered the only organised road-racing in the county. The fact that one of the League's top riders was Geoff Wiles, a former British Champion well into his 60s who sported a hearing aid, said something about that branch of the sport.

As one Kent League rider told me: 'You'll roll up on a Sunday morning, get to the start area and ask Geoff how he's feeling. He'll say he's not too good and doesn't expect to do anything that day. Then the flag drops and after 50km or so he'll just leave you behind. I'm not quite half his age, but it is pretty demoralising.'

Which isn't to disrespect Wiles, an inspirational figure who demonstrated, as did a number of other 'senior' riders, that age counts for less in cycling than in some other sports.

But the standard of racing was reflected by the numbers of spectators these races did, or rather did not, attract. Which made it clear that a Kent stage of the Tour de France had the potential to flop alarmingly.

Chapter 2

AN ACCIDENT OF GEOGRAPHY

When it came to attracting the Tour de France, geography proved to be the county's trump card. There had been rumours and reports of the Tour returning to England for a number of years and these were given a new impetus when Ken Livingstone was elected Mayor of London in 2000. Livingstone may have polarised political opinion more than any other British politician of his era, but he unarguably brought an understanding of the importance of sport and sporting events to his new position. He backed an abortive plan to stage a Formula 1 Grand Prix in the capital, but he was a key player in the successful 2012 Olympic bid and equally supportive of a proposal to bring a stage of the Tour to London.

If the Tour was coming to London, the quickest way for it to get back to France overland would be via Kent, hence the rumours that a London prologue would be followed by a road stage, probably to Canterbury. This was confirmed on 9 February 2006 at a press conference at the QEII centre in central London.

At the time I was the sports editor of the *Kent Messenger* and for a local sports hack, this was not a regular assignment. Anybody who thinks the job is in any way glamourous should spend a shift on an average regional weekly. Sean Dooley, a former regional editor, summed up the lot of the average provincial journalist when he wrote in *The Guardian*: 'Even in the good times my standard promise was to start juniors on a pathetic salary with the proviso that if they worked hard by the end of training it may have progressed to merely disgraceful.'

In the seven years I spent in the job, I saw at least a dozen fresh-faced journalism students turn into embittered refugees who bailed out of the industry to embark on careers in PR, policing and yak farming.

Yet the reason I carried on was for days like this. In Kent we did not have a Premier League football or rugby side to cover, but after hour upon hour of writing about non-League football, darts tournaments and compiling petanque tables, here was a global event landing potentially right on our doorsteps.

I was in London to discover precisely whose doorsteps.

The QEII hall was full of people who could genuinely be called stars in the world of cycling, walking around largely unmolested by around 500 dignitaries who, in most cases, had no idea who they were. For example, Chris Boardman is God to some UK cycling fans, but to the community editor of a local rag in Bexley, who wouldn't know a sprocket from a WMD, he is about as famous as the bass player from Shed Seven.

Bradley Wiggins, despite winning more Olympic medals than Boardman, had an even lower profile, though it was difficult not to notice Paul Kimmage, the former Irish professional who wrote *A Rough Ride*, a seminal account of how cycling's drug culture forced him to give up the sport. Nearly two decades after the book's publication, Kimmage can still be relied on to churn out brilliantly written articles, fired by righteous anger, for *The Sunday Times*, but it must be difficult to live with his level of bile. His sheer puce-ness meant he stuck out a mile, unlike the gaunt figure of former England football international and leukaemia survivor Geoff Thomas, who had cycled the entire route of the Tour after beating

The official start at Greenwich.

Go, go, go! Some riders start their computers at the beginning of the stage.

his illness and now looked about a third of the size he was when he ran Crystal Palace's midfield.

This game of cycle celebrity-spotting continued in the auditorium, where flunkies handed out simultaneous translation units and carrier bags that were filled with entirely frivolous freebies that nonetheless somehow boosted my self-esteem.

The downside of this level of journalism then revealed itself. While the regional hack's job is to churn out stories with the speed and finesse of a sausage machine, the national reporter has to sit through what seems like an eon of public relations sycophantic drivel and diplomatic mutual pleasuring to get to the story and the handful of quotes he or she needs.

Livingstone took to the stage and began with a tribute to departing race director Jean Marie Leblanc. I doubt the pair had met more than twice in their entire lives and yet, to listen to Livingstone's elegy, you would have thought Leblanc had been godfather to the mayor's children.

Leblanc, visibly moved, returned the compliment with a tribute of his own, though frankly it would have been easier for everyone involved if the pair of them had just got a room.

Once the rest of us had been treated as gooseberries for long enough Leblanc exited stage right and his successor, Christian Prudhomme, got to the point.

Photograph courtesy Mike Flynn/Jamie Webb

Discovery's George
Hincapie, sporting the
Stars and Stripes jersey he
wore as champion of the
USA.

He announced that the prologue, or rather Le Grand Depart, would indeed be staged in London on 7 July, but, more pertinently from the *KM's* point of view, he revealed that the route for stage one would be from London to Canterbury, 203km or 126 miles in old money.

Initially at least it sounded like a strategic rather than a scenic route. The riders would parade down Northumberland Avenue and go back and forth over an assortment of bridges before a second, ceremonial 'start' on Tower Bridge.

This was all very pretty, but it would mean that to get to the garden of England, a route through the badlands of south-east London was needed. The official startline was in Greenwich, necessitating a trip through Bermondsey and Deptford, not necessarily the kind of places you would want to be ambling through at walking pace, even with a police escort.

Once the flag dropped, the pack would bomb along the A206 through Charlton, Woolwich and Plumstead before reaching the suburb of Erith, or 'Air-Eeeef' as Prudhomme called it.

There was, however, an element of heroism about Prudhomme's refusal to even try to pronounce the place names properly. In some ways it echoed Charles de Gaulle's refusal to speak English, even though he understood it perfectly well, could produce a Clouseau-esque accent in an emergency and was quite happy to turn his hand to Spanish when he felt like it. After all, the English never made an effort to learn any other language, so why should he put himself out? And whose race was this anyway?

But, back to the Tour. Still on the A206, the riders would arrive in 'DartFORD', birthplace of 'Meek Jaggurr' and into Gravesend, before the first sprint at 'JeelleengAM'. Then the route would head south to my home town, Maidstone (I had to suppress a cheer at this point) and down the A26 to the second sprint at 'TEST-on', then through Hadlow to 'TonBREEDGE' and the first climb of the Tour, Quarry Hill.

Then it would be 'TonBREEDGE Whales' and the next climb at 'GOOODERRST', where the riders would rejoin the 1994 race route – in reverse, though – to the next sprint at 'TentAIRden', 'AshFOORD' and up the final climb of Farthing Common before the finish line in 'ContAirBaiRee'.

It was all I needed to know. With an hour until deadline I had the story but needed some quotes from a local perspective, and while the auditorium was crammed with former Tour riders, as far as I knew only one, Sean Yates, had even a single tenuous connection with Kent (his training routes from his Ashdown Forest home used to take him out as

Fans at the official start line in Greenwich.

Photograph courtesy KM Group

far as Ashford). And he was nowhere to be seen. So I rang Gary Chalkley, co-owner of the Maidstone-based Kent Cycles Racing Team and told him the news that the Tour was going to be flying past his shop.

'I'm speechless!' he replied, which was not entirely what I wanted to hear, but he regained his composure to say: 'You'll put it better than I will. Just say something about it being great news and that hopefully it will stimulate interest in cycling.'

So I did. This is not as journalistically dubious as it sounds – if you have a strong relationship with a contact, he or she will sometimes give you poetic licence to add a little colour to their quotes. If they are OK with the end product this is not considered a problem, although there are obvious pitfalls.

This was pretty safe territory, however. You could not go too far wrong with the story of the bike shop owner who finds out the Tour de France is coming to his front porch.

In one respect, however, I did feel like a small-time Charlie. Almost every other hack in the building had a functioning laptop computer, whereas I had a notepad and a mobile phone. I had to skulk away to a remote corner where nobody would notice I was phoning in the story – a very second-millennium way of working.

The tour makes its official start, a rolling start through Greenwich.

Photograph courtesy KM Group

Chapter 3

DOVER TO BRIGHTON

The Tour de France's trip to England in 2007 was actually the third time the race had crossed the Channel and the results of the previous two trips could not have provided a greater contrast. The French generously shared their annual showpiece with their neighbours, to the point that a race without a border crossing into Italy, Spain, Belgium or Germany had become a rarity by the time they first decided to preach to the unconverted in the UK in 1974.

Yet from almost every conceivable angle it was a disaster.

Logically, the race should have been staged at the closest point to France, i.e. Kent, or at a major population centre in the south, i.e. London, and it should have showcased the spectacular scenery of the region, i.e the North and South Downs, the Seven Sisters and the Weald. Instead the organisers opted to hold the stage in Devon, on a newly-constructed bypass outside Plymouth – and nowhere else. The peloton went from one end of the road to the other and back again, and again, and again *ad nauseum*, until everyone, not least the riders themselves, was bored into submission.

The course could only have appealed to the kind of dyed-in-the-wool time-trialists who follow what passes for racing in Britain. It certainly did not appeal to either the public or the riders, though it did spawn the *Daily Mirror* headline, 'Can 40 million Frenchmen be Wrong?'

Even the winner was a nondescript Dutchman, Henrik Poppe, and with this final stamp of mediocrity the race departed via a ferry to Brittany, not to return for another 20 years.

The lessons of this fiasco were heeded by the time the Tour returned in 1994, though two decades on the sport had evolved and not always in the most edifying of ways.

Cycling slowly succumbed to globalisation. Previously the reserve of a Western European clique, the traditional powerhouses of the sport, France, Belgium, Italy and Spain, saw their stranglehold threatened by a group of English-speaking riders in one direction and the Eastern bloc from the other. The jokers in the pack arrived from Colombia, a nation of mountain goats who regarded the Alps as pimples, but were never able to come to terms with the brutal speeds on the flat stages or the spatial problems posed by riding in a field of 200 riders with everyone cramped elbow-to-elbow and brake-hood-to-buttock.

The single greatest change to the sport in the UK was Channel 4's decision to start screening daily highlights in 1986, having experimented with a weekly package the year before. That year's duel between America's Greg LeMond and his teammate, the reigning champion, France's Bernard Hinault, had everything, including a Prost/Senna-style internal team dynamic, accusations of sabotage, Lemond riding through a bout of diarrhoea and ultimately the sight of the two men metaphorically kissing and making up when they rode arm in arm to the summit of Alpe d'Huez, with LeMond, knowing that the overall win was in the bag, allowing Hinault the consolation prize of a stage win.

It was a symbolic moment in any number of ways, most glaringly because the French have had to feed on scraps ever since. It also succeeded in snaring a generation of new British fans for cycling and a year later thousands more were hooked.

British fans soon adopted Ireland's Stephen Roche as one of their own and his astonishing fightback at La Plagne, where the Spaniard Pedro Delgado had all but left him for dead, remains a seminal moment for legions of cycling fans, not least because of Phil Liggett's commentary: 'Remember at one point the lead was a minute and a half…and just who is that rider coming up behind because it looks like Roche…that looks like Stephen Roche…it is Stephen Roche!'

Liggett's words are seared into my skull.

It was cycling's 'They think it's all over' moment, a piece of broadcasting that has become as famous as the act it described, rivalling Brian Moore's 'It's up for grabs now!' or Barry Davies's 'Where were the Germans, but frankly who cares?'

Twelve months on we watched again, horrified but riveted, as Robert Millar blew the chance of a stage win when he went the wrong way a few hundred metres from the summit of Guzet Neige. It was devastating, but also compelling – this kind of thing just did not happen in the sports I was used to, though as I was to find out 18 years later, it was amazing how easily incidents like this could take place in bike racing.

But by 1988 the first serious dark clouds were also looming on the horizon.

With Roche and LeMond both absent Delgado was cruising to victory when a dope test revealed he had taken probenicide, a masking agent. Delgado escaped censure on what now seems like a laughable technicality – the UCI had not got round to banning it.

It begged an obvious question – what was Delgado masking? The question was ignored by Spanish fans, who regarded 'Perico' as a demi-god, perhaps because there was nothing new in doping, or, to call it by its proper name, cheating, in the Tour de France.

In 1904, the race's second year, so many riders tried to pervert the course of the race by the unsubtle method of catching the train that the race founder, Henri Desgranges, considered killing the event off after just two years.

Two decades later the Pélissier brothers, Francis and Henri, well and truly let the cat out of the bag.

Abandoning the race after a dispute with the race organisers, Henri treated the journalist Albert Londres to the scoop of a lifetime:

'You have no idea what the Tour de France is like. It is martyrdom. And even the Way of the Cross had only 14 stations, while we have 15 stages. We suffer from start to finish. Do you want to see how we walk? Here. Hold this.' At this point he produced his chemistry set. 'That, it is cocaine

The usually traffic-choked A206 at Woolwich.

Photograph courtesy KM Group

for the eyes, that it is chloroform for the gums, that is pomade, meant to heat my knees. And the pills? Do you want to see the pills? Here. Hold the pills.'

The brothers handed Londres three boxes of pills each, before Francis said, 'In short, we walk with dynamite.'

Henri then decided to cut in: 'You did not see us before we bathed upon arrival. When we scrape the mud off, we are white like shrouds, the diarrhoea drains us, we shed tears. In the evening, in bed in our rooms, we do the dance of Saint Guy instead of sleeping. Look at our laces, they are made of leather. They never hold, they always break, and it is tanned leather that bleeds when wet. Think of what that does to our skin. When we are thrown from the machine, the shock passes through our socks, through our breeches, and nothing protects our bodies.'

Francis interrupted, 'the meat falls off our skeletons.'

And Henri concluded, 'and as for my nails, I lost six out of ten. They die gradually in each stage.'

Like Henri's nails, as it entered the 1990s, cycling was about to suffer a gradual death, with Delgado's tarnished win just an hors d'oeuvres for the horrors that followed.

The damage, however, was not immediately apparent. The 1989 Tour de France was one of the greatest races ever, with LeMond recovering

David Millar, far left, makes his move on Plumstead High Street, yards from the site of Arsenal FC's old Manor Ground.

from a near-fatal shooting accident he had suffered two years previously to beat France's Laurent Fignon by just eight seconds after the final time trial on the Champs Elysées. LeMond won again in 1990, but in 1991 he was dethroned in spectacular fashion by Miguel Indurain as a new era began.

Indurain's style was so tedious that he was to cycling what Jose Mourinho's unlovable but overwhelming Chelsea side would be to football, but the real problem remained hidden at that point.

By the early 1990s the market was flooded with undetectable doping products that propelled riders to previously undreamt-of speeds. Just how many riders were using drugs remains open to debate, but the evidence overwhelmingly points to a peloton in which clean riders were an endangered species, making it difficult to take any result from 1991 onwards seriously.

There were multiple casualties. A spate of deaths occurred as riders' blood clotted in their veins, stopping their hearts.

Clean riders, like Chris Boardman and Charly Mottet, were robbed of the careers they should have had, their sporadic victories proving isolated triumphs against the cheats.

The former world hour record holder Graeme Obree, subject of the film *The Flying Scotsman*, had his illusions shattered by a teammate who told him that a portion of his newly-awarded professional contract would be requisitioned by the team for 'medical back-up'.

In some cases the riders did not even realise they were cheating. The Australian Neil Stephens told the journalist James Startt how one of his victories seemed too good to be true, because, it gradually dawned on him, it was. As part of the Festina squad, Stephens was asked to attend police questioning in Lyon. He did so voluntarily, only to suffer a 24-hour nightmare. Stripped naked, given the rubber-glove treatment and forced to walk barefoot through other people's urine to go to the toilet, Stephens's statement was eventually believed – that he had simply trusted his team doctors and did not question what they were putting into his veins.

Later on he was forced to admit to himself he had been wrong to put his faith in men who supposedly adhered to the hippocratic oath: 'You know, when you're in the Tour you're getting injections all the time. They say you can't drink enough, so you get IVs. Plus you're getting amino acid supplements, tablets, all sorts of things. A doctor is paid 5,000 francs a day to look after you, so you trust him.'

Stephens initially insisted his own experience was proof that you could ride the Tour and be clean. But when Startt reminded him he had actually won a stage in 1997, it seemed to shatter something inside the Australian: 'I'd like to think there was nothing going on, but you've got to know. Same doctor, same staff.' The Euro had dropped for Stephens.

Ironically, his teammate Richard Virenque, one of the least repentant cheats, had inadvertently won a stage 'clean' when his masseur, Willy Voet, gave him a placebo instead of the rocket fuel he had requested.

Others did not ask questions when they were being hooked up to needles, allowing them to 'plausibly deny' any suggestion of cheating, though for many riders doping was simply a question of professionalism. Corrupt doctors were co-opted onto teams to allow riders to dope while 'minimising' the risk to their health.

This was an obvious fallacy.

By 1996 the Tour de France had become a three-week game of Russian roulette. The key to winning the race used to be endurance, but the upside of EPO (erythropoietin) was that it allowed riders to ride themselves into the ground every day and begin the next morning as fresh as a daisy.

The downside was that it killed you. If the pulse rate fell below a certain level, a cyclist could die in his sleep as the treacle-like blood would stop flowing and the heart would cease to beat.

Riders would set their alarms for 3am, get up and start pedalling on rollers, just to prevent cardiac arrest. Yet amazingly so many agreed to this pact with the devil that by 1996 some of the peloton had blood like a nice and water slush. A haematocrit level of 40 per cent is considered average. At 50 per cent the authorities would later 'invite' you to stop racing for your own protection – in 1996 some riders were pushing 60 per cent.

The tell-tale signs were there. Denmark's Bjarne Riis, previously a journeyman pro, won the 1996 race at the age of 32. A year later Jan Ullrich, one of the last products of the notorious East German regime, followed suit. The achievements of both men would later be discredited – though in Ullrich's case this was more of a tragedy as he was widely recognised to have more talent than any other rider of his generation – but for a decade they got away with it.

Thus when the Tour came to Britain for its second visit in 1994, the sport remained a saleable commodity and the organisers heeded the lessons of the 1974 failure.

Chapter 4

LATRINE DUTY

In July 1994 I had just completed a year as a student in Strasbourg, the beer capital of France. I was supposed to be studying politics, but I devoted as much time, if not more, to researching the effects of cheap Alsatian ale. My French became fluent, but I observed rather than absorbed the local culture and when I was not imbibing in a room the size of a rabbit hutch with expat Brits, Irish and Americans I found my preconceived ideas of France being challenged.

In some cases they were reinforced, in others obliterated.

They did not know how to drive, they were laughably bureaucratic and they were rude – indeed, in Alsace, rudeness seemed to be as much of a regional speciality as the one franc bottles of Munsterhof we used to drink in emergencies. For all the French tend to resent people who do

Andreas Kloden (far left, in the green jersey) leads the bunch around a roundabout on the A206 in Erith, or 'Air-eef' as it was known to the French race organisers.

Photograph courtesy KM Group

25

not speak their language, when someone actually makes an effort some of them enjoy playing a little game called: 'Try to make the foreigner feel inferior by pretending not to understand.' Thus you ask for some batteries for your camera and are met with a look that straddles quizzical and irritated. After repeating the word for batteries four times, the shop assistant finally pretends she hasn't understood you all along and says, 'Ah, des piles…' at which point you fight the urge to reply: 'If you're so superior then why, precisely, are you working behind the counter of a camera shop?'

In Alsace counter staff took this transparently feeble psychology to a new level, by communicating with each other in French and then addressing you in Alsatian dialect the moment you attempted to interrupt them by deigning to give them some custom.

Again, one had to fight the temptation to reply: 'Yes, we both know that I don't understand what you just said, but let's dispense with the idea that because you speak what is basically German with a ludicrously see-saw accent you are in some way my intellectual and moral superior. Now serve me.'

Other illusions were steadily shattered. You could eat well, if you were rich, but as penniless students you either had to join the trough at the 'Resto-Universitaires' or exist on pasta, chocolate and beer.

Women were no more available than their British counterparts, despite Gene Hackman only having to look at a volleyball player on Marseille beach to get her in the sack in *French Connection 2*, and I saw little evidence that cycling was any more popular in France than it was in England.

On my excursions into the surrounding countryside, through villages with typically French names like Niederhausbergen and Lingolsheim, I came across fewer lycra-clad riders than

Spectators gather in Erith to watch the 2007 Tour de France pass through the town, heading for Canterbury, on the first stage of the gruelling three-week event.

Photograph courtesy KM Group

The pack passes the Orchard Theatre in Dartford, birthplace of the man the French call 'Meek Jaggurr'.

I would riding around Maidstone. As a sport, cycling struggled to drag the limelight away from football (even though the country was still in the throes of the Marseille match-fixing saga), Formula 1 and rugby.

Paris-Roubaix, which I believed to be the world's greatest one-day bike race, received about the same amount of media coverage as the Boat Race would in England and the Tour de France was only a topic of conversation once – when my mother rang to ask if I wanted to be a steward when the race passed through Kent.

Wanting to get involved, I agreed and pitched up at Cranbrook police station on the morning of the stage to report for duty. I sat through the *Hill Street Blues*-style police briefing, was handed an IQ-reducing yellow jacket and dropped off at Goudhurst, or more specifically the junction of Lovers Lane and the B2084 to Horsmonden.

It was like being assigned latrine-duty. The stewards for our stretch of the route had been allocated positions by the Southborough Wheelers Cycling Club and understandably they had cherry-picked the best vantage points for their members.

The bunch cross the Crayford/Dartford border and enter Kent proper.

As the only organisation I belonged to at that point was the great unwashed, I found myself patrolling a 50-metre stretch of road, meaning I could see 25 metres in one direction and 25 in another. Although Goudhurst's centre boasts some of the most spectacular views in Kent, all I could see was tarmac, a wall and a few hedgerows. To make matters worse my only company was a policeman, whose initial bonhomie subsided over the course of several hours to reveal a sub-Littlejohn mentality to all things foreign.

Neither of us had anything to do, though at one point a local pensioner asked when he would be able to get out of his drive, giving my companion the chance to do his Inspector Knacker routine, generally being obnoxious and then scampering for the moral high ground at the first whiff of any indignation.

At least an hour went by before we saw the first race vehicles and then a mind-numbing procession of media cars and publicity trucks followed, decorated with giant apples and spewing leaflets and mini-flags into the hedgerows.

After another hour the commentator, Hugh Porter, arrived, telling us two riders had broken away from the main field. A gaggle of motorbikes went by and there they were, Francisco Cabello of the Kelme team and Castorama's Emmanuel Magnien. They were in my field of vision for perhaps 30 seconds, probably less. More motorbikes went past, their two team cars followed and around five minutes later the main field loomed into view, before quickly looming out of it. It was a mesmerising sight, or at least it would have been had it lasted longer than the time it takes to munch down a chocolate bar.

I recognised just two riders. Miguel Indurain, barely breaking sweat, was chatting to one of his followers and the hefty, pre-cancer figure of Lance Armstrong in the World Champion's rainbow jersey could also be made out.

And then they were gone, the broom wagon trailing in their wake.

Several hours invested in a few seconds of live action. It had not cost me anything, but I was a cycling fan, so how would the uninitiated feel about it?

The public voted, emphatically, with their feet. Estimates of the crowd vary, but it seems at least one million people lined the route, with an equivalent or greater number watching the following day's stage in Hampshire. If their race experience was as truncated as mine, it didn't register in their facial expressions, nor did the majority of them really care who was out in front.

Yet Cabello and Magnien were virtual unknowns in the UK, which, by 1994, needed a serious Tour challenger, someone who could snare a new generation of fans and racers.

Only two Britons had ever looked like even outside contenders for the yellow jersey and the first of them, Tom Simpson, haunted the sport. The epithet 'tragic' was only too appropriate for Simpson, the most naturally gifted all-rounder the country had ever produced and the only British rider ever to win the World Road Race Championship.

Simpson's doomed attempts to win the Tour eventually killed him. As he

The Tour's official Supermarket, Champion - yet to expand into the Gravesend area.

Photograph courtesy KM Group

Not a design for traditionalists.

attempted to climb Mont Ventoux in 1967, having ingested a cocktail of amphetamines and alcohol, his heart stopped and he collapsed at the roadside.

His alleged last words, 'put me back on my bike' entered cycling folklore, but according to his biographer William Fotheringham he never actually said them. Instead he merely begged his mechanic to be allowed to continue, slurring the word 'on' before completing a few more pedal strokes, then keeling over.

In 1984 Robert Millar won the King of the Mountains title and finished fourth overall. A year later he was effectively cheated out of the Tour of Spain by a nefarious pact between home riders, but his second-place finish – and a strong claim to be the race's moral victor – suggested that with a following wind he could win the Tour de France. However, the wind never followed Millar and his subsequent Tours were dogged by bad luck, injury and the dawning realisation that the best he could hope for would be the odd stage win and top 10 finish.

His King of the Mountains title in 1984 remained the high watermark for Millar and to this day his fourth place overall has never been bettered by a British cyclist. Nor does it seem likely that Millar's feat will be matched or bettered in the near future, although in the early 1990s the emergence of Chris Boardman as a world-class rider allowed fans to dream that they might finally have a genuine Tour contender.

Having won the 1992 Olympic Pursuit Gold Medal, the articulate Boardman (on his space-age time-trial bike) was far easier to market than the notoriously surly Millar, and when he defied his own expectations to win the 1994 Tour de France prologue in Lille he became the first British rider to wear the yellow jersey since Simpson. He retained it for three stages, but lost it when his GAN team put in a lamentably incoherent performance in the team time trial, held on a circuit at Cap Gris Nez, the closest part of mainland Europe to England.

The proximity of the White Cliffs of Dover initially worsened Boardman's sense of anguish at having lost the jersey, but he quickly got over it.

This time the race organisers had chosen a route that showcased everything the south of England had to offer. From the spectacular backdrop of Dover Castle, all the way through to Brighton, Boardman was given rock star treatment by the roadside hordes.

Magnien and Cabello went on the attack early on and stayed away for almost the entire stage, but as virtual unknowns their attack did not ignite the crowds. They built their lead on Stone Street, a Roman road with panoramic views across the Stour Valley, increased it through Canterbury and Ashford, held it comfortably as they flitted past my field of vision in Goudhurst and continued into Tunbridge Wells and Sussex.

A fan of Lance Armstrong's defunct US Postal team, complete with giant foam hand, in Gravesend.

Britain's other rider, Forest Row's superdomestique Sean Yates, was allowed a short lead by the peloton as the race entered the Ashdown Forest, a tradition afforded local riders so that they can say hello to their relatives, but as the race neared Brighton the chase began in earnest.

Ditchling Beacon was temporarily transformed, with thousands of cycling fans making it look more like Alpe D'Huez than a second category ascent of the South Downs, barely 200 metres high, though it is worth remembering Robert Millar's verdict when asked about Ditchling after tackling it in a previous World Cup race:

'What did you think of the hill Robert?'

'What hill?'

Photograph courtesy KM Group

Boardman's initial regret at not being able to ride the stage in the yellow jersey evaporated as the peloton hit the streets of Brighton. Flavio Vanzella shot out of the bunch and Boardman, fêted like a Beatle in *A Hard Day's Night*, sped after him as the race went up Elm Grove, a slope that resembles a cliff-face, on the finishing circuit.

It was, he later confessed, an 'ego trip'. Although Vanzella held off the peloton and actually managed to overhaul Magnien, Cabello had ditched his long-time partner and held on for the win.

Boardman did not have the legs to reel in the top three, but he held off the bunch and broke with convention by raising both arms to celebrate his fourth place. His exuberance may have been frowned upon in the peloton, but given the reception he had received from the public he could hardly be blamed for getting carried away.

Selling garlic in Gravesend.

Watching, captivated, from the road side, was a teenage Scot named David Millar. Boardman's exploits inspired Millar – no relation to Robert, but in his own way an equally complex and fascinating character – to begin his cycling career.

Sadly he was an exceptional case. British riders trickled, rather than flooded, to the Continent and it quickly became apparent that Boardman, despite a promising ride in the mountains in the 1995 Dauphine Libère, was never going to be an overall contender – though given a level (i.e. drug-free) playing field, things might have been different.

Television coverage if anything dwindled in the years that followed, with the race disappearing from terrestrial screens altogether after 2000.

Photograph courtesy KM Group

I, meanwhile, got back to Maidstone in time to see the race unfold from Ditchling onwards and came to the conclusion that cycling was one of those sports, like motor racing, best enjoyed in front of a television set.

And I had not yet realised that much of what I and over a million others had witnessed had been a charade.

Allez! Tour de France at Gravesend, New Road and King Street.

Chapter 5

BLOOD MONEY

A few months after the Tour de France's second visit to Kent in 2007, the sports editor of a rival newspaper confessed to me that he had advocated ignoring the race completely. He was happy for pictures of giant dogs on lorries and children with painted faces to go in the news section, but as far as he was concerned, the scandals of the previous decade had stripped the race itself of any integrity.

Although rumours of blood-doping had been flying around for years it was not until 1998 that the *merde* had finally hit the fan.

Willy Voet, a previously unknown masseur and ham doctor, was arrested trying to cross the border between Belgium and France days before the start of the race, in a car that contained the Festina team's entire doping arsenal. He sang like a canary, and with the Festina squad's position in the race untenable, they were expelled, to a chorus of indignation from their riders, particularly Virenque. As the investigation widened and the police closed in on fresh suspects, team after team pulled out and there was talk of abandoning the race altogether.

This might have been preferable to the eventual outcome, which saw the rump of the peloton led home by the Italian Marco Pantani, a cyclist whose fate put Ullrich's tragedy in the shade.

Like Ullrich, Pantani had raw natural talent, but unlike Ullrich he specialised in the high mountains, winning Alpine stages with the kind of panache the German was derided for lacking. There was common ground, however. Despite their god-given ability, neither felt they could compete without using, as they saw it, the best medical help they could get, and neither was prepared to ride clean and be beaten by a doped rival.

Ullrich largely got away with it until he fell foul of Operation Puerto in 2006, but Pantani's fall from grace came in the 1999 Tour of Italy, when, with overall victory assured, he was ejected from the race after his red blood cell count exceeded the 50 per cent maximum limit.

This was not proof in itself that he had been blood doping, however. As Robert Millar later pointed out, the red blood cell count should go down rather than up in a three-week stage race.

It is possible, probable even, that Pantani was in denial – his fans clearly were – but his refusal to accept any responsibility for his plight saw his life enter a self-pitying tailspin that culminated in his death from a cocaine overdose in 2004.

The extent of Pantani's drug abuse was later revealed by his Kent-born biographer Matt Rendell, but the reaction to Rendell's book only served to illustrate the crisis cycling was in. Rendell was subjected to a sustained campaign of vilification in Italy, a country he subsequently confessed to 'falling out of love' with. He received death threats from fans who felt that investigative journalism was in some way a greater crime than sporting fraud and drug abuse.

Millar builds his lead through Gravesend.

Pantani's rivals, with a few honourable exceptions, were as happy as his fanatical devotees to carry on ignoring the extent of the problem, but the fans who had been thrilled by LeMond and Roche now regarded cycling as little more than a competition between doctors.

It was like dumping gallon after gallon of toxic waste into a river. The Tour survived for the time being, but for how long would this river be able to sustain life?

For a time a good news story eclipsed the scandals. From 1999 to 2005 the race was won on seven consecutive occasions by Lance Armstrong, whose inspirational fight-back from cancer transcended mere sport.

Yet every time cycling seemed to be making a tentative recovery, another tawdry episode sent its image tumbling back into the gutter.

Gravesend as it has never been seen before – or since.

Armstrong certainly did not help himself, with his boorish behaviour towards some of his rivals, and his association with the controversial Italian doctor Michele Ferrari left him wide open to accusations that he had something to hide. But the feeling persisted that a section of the French cycling community regarded Armstrong's domination of 'their' event as even more invidious than the Festina scandal, and there was a hint of desperation in the assaults on the Texan's reputation by the media.

The mud stuck, however. In 2002, while on holiday in Provence, a friend and I cycled from Antibes to Vence, and halfway up the 1,000m Col de Vence we stopped to refill our bidons in the town square. As we rested for 20 minutes before setting out for the summit, a 70-year-old Frenchman sat next to us and began to give us his unsolicited views on the sport.

'Les Americains ont perfecté le dopage,' he lectured us, accusing the US Postal Service team in particular of a ruthlessly effective programme that administered scientifically undetectable quantities of drugs to enable its riders to beat the (French) competition. His pious standpoint might have been a little easier to accept if he had not, in the next breath, extolled the virtues of his own favourite rider, Fausto Coppi, the campionissimo.

If there were doubts about Armstrong's medical history, there were none at all about Coppi's. The man himself had replied 'only when necessary' when asked if he had taken amphetamines. But when was it necessary? 'Almost always', Coppi admitted.

Jacques Anquetil, a five-time Tour de France winner, had been almost as honest when he said that the public were deluded if they believed the Tour could be won on mineral water.

How could the French laud Coppi, Anquetil and, worst of all, Virenque when they knew they were guilty, while excoriating Armstrong who, according to the strictest doping control programme ever devised, was innocent?

His training regime was a matter of public knowledge. When other riders were partying through the winter, Armstrong was riding for seven hours at a time, repeatedly scaling the climbs he would have to ride in the Tour, mentally taking notes on every change in the gradient, every potentially lethal hairpin and every launchpad for a stage-winning attack.

The whole thing smacked of residual anti-Americanism from World War Two. The French had long since forgiven the Germans for the occupation, but had not yet managed to pardon the Americans for the liberation. The French did not, however, have a monopoly on double standards, with the British cycling media proving equally adroit at straddling the moral divide. The cycling Press repeatedly carried articles, editorials and letters pillorying riders for doping, but continued to refer to known drug cheats as champions while also carrying adverts for videos celebrating the careers of Pantani, Coppi, Ullrich et al.

But then, the Tour nurtured hypocrisy. Ethical ambivalence was the inevitable consequence of reporting on race after race, year after year, that turned out to be a sham.

In his memoir *Bad Blood*, the former editor of *Procycling Magazine* Jeremy Whittle described his own passage over to the dark side when a rider he interviewed accidentally dropped some spent contraband in front of him. 'You weren't supposed to see that Jeremy,' he said, somewhat feebly, and Whittle, knowing the rider was a family man who doped to keep up rather than win, felt unable to turn him in.

Some felt the only morally correct course of action was to ignore cycling completely, yet even the sport's fiercest critic, the former professional cyclist Paul Kimmage, now of *The Sunday Times*, repeatedly

The bunch is funneled
through Gravesend's
narrow pedestrian area.

The CSC team in Gravesend.

finds himself drawn back to the Tour, because, as he put it: 'I love the event, I hate the people who've ruined it.'

And as Matt Rendell pointed out, cycling remained headline news: 'Because it's such a great story.' He was right. Cycling had become almost like politics. Even when the scandals became so regular that they were at the point of saturating the public's appetite for hard news, there was still a journalistic thrill at exposing, for example, Ivan Basso's part in Operation Puerto, just as a political correspondent would get a tingle when he got wind of John Prescott's affair or 'Lord' Archer's perjury.

It would hardly be surprising if *Cycling Weekly*'s editorial crew had been left dizzy as scandal after scandal unfolded in front of them, but the credibility of the Tour had been eroded to the point that when the race itself arrived in Britain, there was a serious risk that the sporting angle would be ignored.

Kent's sports journalists could roughly be divided into three camps. Some were avowed and unrepentant fans, some were completely indifferent and others were openly hostile, though it belatedly dawned on most of them that, drugs or no drugs, if several hundred thousand people were about to witness an event in their back garden, they had better at least make sure it got more coverage than the annual Faversham Bowls Tournament. BBC Kent were so keen that someone even

Photograph courtesy KM Group

The CSC team in Gravesend.

volunteered to drive and film the entire route, before putting footage of his road trip on the corporation's website and giving it a soundtrack (inevitably, *Tour de France* by Kraftwerk).

All leave was cancelled and a 40-strong team was assembled to cover the weekend.

Yet sports editor Matt Davison admitted that they saw it as a social occasion as opposed to a sporting contest.

Davison, who covered the 1994 stage from a race car, was typical of many fans, interested in the Tour and the Olympics but not a cycling aficionado:

'I was always a fan of the Tour de France,' he told me. 'But I don't think many people would deny that there was always that nagging doubt at the back of your mind. I remembered some of the races I'd watched in the past and felt a little bit like I'd been cheated. So it wasn't so much a cycling event for me – more of a party.'

At the *Kent & Sussex Courier* they were similarly ambivalent about the race, but three members of the sports desk decided they would physically ride the entire route and two of them actually made it, the third bailing out after reaching Ashford, which was still some achievement.

At the *Kent Messenger*, however, I was the unofficial cycling correspondent and most of my colleagues willingly left me to it.

As the race day drew nearer and more of my time was devoted to covering it, they began to press me on the sport's integrity, and the epithet 'Tour de Drug' was coined. The expression 'Tour de Pharmacie' was also used and I shall spare readers the knowledge of any further gems, for fear they may die laughing.

It was a bit like being stuck in a pub next to a man who thinks that because he's had six pints of Spitfire he is a reincarnation of Tommy Cooper.

I had heard all the accusations before and was not about to act as an apologist for the Tour's failings.

As a defence lawyer I would have been sacked on the spot, but rather than defend the indefensible I went on the counter-attack, lacerating my peers for their own double standards. For me, taking illegal drugs was cheating – cheating the public, your fellow professionals and ultimately yourself if your ill-gotten gains were offset by crippling health problems later in life. But we were all football and cricket fans in the office and

Kuchynski leads the chase.

Photograph courtesy KM Group

cheating was endemic to both those sports. In the average football season I would watch around 50 live matches and hundreds more on television. In every single one of them the players knowingly cheated, their offences ranging from appealing for throw-ins when they knew they had put the ball out of play, to two-footed assaults on opponents masquerading as tackles.

Then there was Didier Drogba. The man was unquestionably a hero. With his fellow countryman Kolo Toure he had helped to negotiate a ceasefire in a civil war in the Ivory Coast. Yet on the field his misdemeanours were, to my mind, as serious as any committed by a cyclist. He may have been a great player, but why did he have to try to pervert the course of football matches? He somehow summoned feelings of outrage whenever his integrity was questioned (à la Richard Virenque), yet every time he fell over in a stiff breeze, Drogba was trying to con someone and get a fellow professional sent off – and he was anything but an exception.

Cricket was arguably even worse, because it sought to occupy the moral high ground.

At least when cyclists cheated they were trying to win. The much-vaunted 'spirit of cricket' was a myth to anyone who had watched a match rigged by Hansie Cronje, seen Mike Atherton rub dirt into the ball or watched an orchestrated appeal by a fielding side who knew the batsman wasn't out.

Rugby loved to lecture other sports on the concept of respecting the officials, but this seemed irrelevant set against the sheer violence players meted out to each other inside and out of the laws of the game. And finally there was golf, where people never cheated, where honour was all important and where sanctimony was only outstripped by sheer tedium.

Chapter 6

WAR

As valid as these arguments were, all they did was erode my faith in other sports, rather than restore any in cycling. The only route back was to see the issue in George W. Bush terms, and after years of appeasement, the cycling authorities belatedly declared war on drugs.

Those of us tortured by the Tour's fate were suffering because we knew it was an event worth saving, and after all – what was the alternative? To give up and abandon the race altogther, the ultimate victory for the cheats?

For ASO, the race organisers, the final straw seemed to be the 2006 race. After seven years of gritting their teeth and applauding Armstrong on the podium, the Texan finally retired after the 2005 Tour and everyone looked forward to an open race. Although Armstrong was by far the most

Fans at Rochester Castle watch on the big screen – the bunch can be seen heading through Strood.

Photograph courtesy KM Group

thrilling racer to watch, he rivalled Indurain when it came to meticulousness and his zero tolerance approach to errors meant he needed to be having a run of bad luck (as in 2003) for his rivals to stand any chance.

In 2006 human error was again a factor in deciding the race. The winner, a decent but by no means outstanding Spanish rider called Oscar Pereiro, profited from the kind of error unheard of during the Armstrong era to break away from the main field on a flat stage. As a respectable climber and time-triallist, Pereiro put enough time between him and his rivals to build a lead he was able to hold through the Alps – though at the time it looked as though it would only be good enough for second place.

Pereiro's main rival was another American, Floyd Landis, who had defied his parents' strict Mennonite upbringing to race bikes for a living. Sadly for Landis's parents, riding his bike when he should have been wearing a 17th-century costume to church was the least of his transgressions.

Landis, who was a Tour favourite despite a degenerative hip condition, cracked so badly on the penultimate Alpine stage that he ended up falling eight minutes behind Pereiro. That night, so he claimed, he drank beer and whisky, again in violation of his parents' Mennonite beliefs, but rather than suffering from a hangover Landis found himself in the form of his life the

Fans watch at Rochester Cathedral and Castle.

Photograph courtesy KM Group

following morning. He launched an astonishing solo attack, riding alone for 130 kilometres and clawing back seven and a half minutes of Pereiro's lead. In the final time trial he overhauled the rest of Pereiro's advantage and the following day he was fêted as the Tour's champion in Paris.

It was an astonishing story, with a solitary flaw. It was total b*llocks.

Four days after Landis's Tour 'win', I learned he was due to ride that September's Tour of Britain with his Phonak team. This was a major story in our part of the world as it meant that an A-list rider would be cycling through Kent. Stage five of the 2006 Tour of Britain was from Rochester to Canterbury and in the (permanent) absence of any hard news, I asked the *Kent Messenger*'s picture editor, Barry Hollis, if he could find us a suitable shot for our back page.

Hollis had so many contacts in the industry that he could get you a picture of Mohandas Gandhi in a Sheppey fish restaurant if you asked him nicely, but for the first time in all my years at the *KM*, he failed to get hold of any images we could use.

I reluctantly filled the back with an alternative story, probably about a netball tournament in Aylesford, went home at the end of my shift and, not really knowing how to wind down, flicked on the television to check the latest sports news.

The crowds laugh, but the driver is wondering how he'll explain this on his CV.

Rochester's town crier goes for a traditional British banger.

It would be an exaggeration to say my blood ran cold when I saw that Landis had failed a drug test, but even after witnessing so many similar scandals I was shocked, and the feeling was only eclipsed by the sense of relief that Hollis had not produced the picture.

Maybe it was karma, more likely it was pure luck. The cycling Press was less fortunate. Earlier deadlines meant that every British cycling magazine had a picture of Landis splashed on its front cover, though one managed to put stickers on its polybags saying that readers should visit their website for the latest news on the Landis case.

The latest news was thus. Landis had failed his A sample after his ride to Morzine. He denied it, as riders always did, but his testosterone level was so high that Dick Pound was moved to comment that he was surprised Landis hadn't deflowered every virgin in the area. It was amateur night. Landis was condemned by the anti-drug crusaders and derided by the dopers for getting caught. Testosterone was anything but a designer drug and using it to win a stage was like robbing a bank and then walking up to the security cameras, whipping off your stocking and grinning for the police.

Chapter 7

DRESS REHEARSAL DISASTER

In the enforced absence of Landis, the star attraction at the 2006 Tour of Britain was the reigning World Champion Tom Boonen, though he would turn into the villain of this particular piece for vastly different reasons.

Comparing the British Tour with its French counterpart is like comparing the World Cup to the Auto Windscreens Shield Final. It was not realistic to demand the same standards in either the organisation or the calibre of the field, but when the news broke that the British event was coming to Kent in September it felt like a bonus – an *amuse bouche* before the main event 10 months later, for which there was already a palpable sense of anticipation building.

It was also a useful dry run. The stage, from Rochester to Canterbury, followed a similar, though not identical, route to the Tour de France, but as the organisers had a budget that was just a fraction of ASO's, there were inevitably going to be headaches.

The announcement of the route was made with so little fanfare it almost slipped through the net completely, though the PR people attempted to redress the balance with a media ride two months before the race.

I could not resist accepting the invitation, even though I had barely trained that summer, and rolled up to a rendezvous point in Rochester High Street at 9am on Monday 17 July.

There were around nine of us: journalists, PR people, Nick Collins, the owner of the DFL cycling team and Tony Doyle, the former World Pursuit Champion, now in his 40s and looking fit, if a few stone heavier than he had been in his prime.

In the early stages of my journalistic career I was overawed by people I regarded as genuine stars, with the cricketer Brian Lara reducing me to

The wrong channel on the big screen.

a shambling wreck, capable only of shoving my notepad in his face to ask for an autograph, as opposed to any saleable quotes.

Out of necessity I eventually overcame this and was happily chatting away to Doyle as if he was an old clubmate as we ambled out of Rochester on the Esplanade and then up the 1 in 7 climb of Shorts Way.

'How much faster would you have ridden that in your pro days?' I asked him.

'Significantly,' he smiled, which I took to mean at least twice the 7mph we managed.

Doyle, it emerged, had a curious relationship with the highway code. His mobile phone rang at 10 minute intervals and he always answered it, even in heavy traffic. The concept of giving way to oncoming vehicles had clearly passed him by too, and he seemed to think that raising an arm, traffic policeman style, would give him priority at roundabouts and make him immune to the impact of an onrushing hulk of metal travelling at 50mph.

We rode along the Pilgrims Way to Aylesford and deliberately deviated from the route at Ditton to head up Kiln Barn Road and avoid the miserable West Malling bypass.

We rejoined the race route at Mereworth and then deviated again, this time accidentally, heading towards Tonbridge on the A26 instead of following the correct route through Paddock Wood. We were in Tonbridge itself before we realised we had gone wrong and there things got even worse.

Not realising there was no slip road to the Hastings-bound A21 from the A26, we ended up going even further off piste through Tunbridge Wells. This put us an hour behind our schedule, and although he struggled on Goudhurst Hill, where Collins left him behind, Doyle effectively towed us all the way to our lunch venue at Small Hythe – though this itself was a further three miles out of our way, making for a six-mile detour on what was probably the hottest day of the summer.

'Cold meat salads all round,' Doyle told the waitress as soon as we entered, which at least spared us the agony of choice, and as we made a partial recovery over ham and lettuce the man from *The Sunday People* entertained us with the gossip on Sven Goran Eriksson.

The oldest trick in the hack book is to ask a contact for their phone number at the end of any interview, 'just in case I need to check anything.' Sven, politely but firmly, would never fall for this, until the day he was interviewed by a young female reporter. Before she could even ask him for his number, the Swede had handed her a card.

The bunch pass Rochester Castle – and unlike in the 2006 Tour of Britain, this year they actually race.

Photograph courtesy KM Group

The journalist also told us how difficult it was getting any kind of cycling story in a national paper: 'The only event anyone has ever heard of is the Tour de France and the only cyclist anyone's heard of is Lance Armstrong, so any story has got to be about him. It can only be 400 words long and you've got to find a way of writing it without mentioning drugs.'

We nearly got a story the moment we left the café. Rolling down the drive I saw a sports car approaching at speed from the south and stopped. Doyle, who was riding behind me, saw it and simply carried on, steering straight into the car's path and causing the driver to slam on the brakes.

'Get some ******* glasses!' the driver yelled, in righteous anger. Doyle tried to placate him, but the driver thrice cursed him before he finally got a response, Doyle eventually saying 'all right, calm down Grandad!'

In Tenterden Doyle was about to take us the wrong way once again and he would have ended up in Romney Marsh if we hadn't yelled after him. Yet without him we would have been three hours late for our arrival party in Canterbury and he again towed us through Ham Street, Bilsington and over Farthing Corner before setting the maximum pace our legs could stand along Stone Street.

The Tour de France would follow this road, a plateau from the summit of the North Downs for half a dozen miles until it dips down into Canterbury. They would average close to 40mph on this stretch. We

It could be a dog...

The riders are either being saluted, or targeted, from Fort Amherst.

managed 17 and that was in Doyle's slipstream. The road to Lympne had softened us up, the hill to Stanford forced the man from *The People* to jump in the broom wagon, while Farthing Corner all but emptied the rest of the tank.

The last few miles reinforced a lesson I had learned long ago. If you wanted to be a competitive, racing cyclist you had to be prepared to suffer like a dog and keep on taking the pain, for hours on end.

This wasn't like football, where you played for 90 minutes and then stopped, tired, but still fresh enough to stand around in a bar dissecting the game. This was a perpetual ordeal, one that drained your body's resources so comprehensively that it left you in a trance, permanently on the brink of exhaustion and wondering just how much longer you could keep going until you toppled into a ditch.

It is a myth to think the professionals simply get used to this. It is one thing having the god-given physique needed to turn the pedals, but unless you have the capacity to endure pain in consistently incrementing doses you don't stand a chance.

On the final approaches to Canterbury, through Street End and along the Nackington Road, I understood why certain riders felt compelled to take drugs. It was easy to see how your mindset could evolve when you had to cope with a sustained physical assault on every moving part of your body, though this merely heightened the sympathy I felt for clean riders who were beaten to the line by dopers.

It was exhausting, exhilarating and also eerily prophetic of Saturday 2 September when the stage itself took place. The previous four stages had been beset by problems, principally with traffic getting onto the race route. These were hinted at by Boonen during the pre-race interviews at Rochester Castle, although he did not actually have the brass neck to tell the spectators what the field had planned for them.

I watched the field roll down the ramp at Rochester Castle oblivious to the mood in the peloton. I walked down to Castle Keep, standing between the castle and cathedral, and along with a healthy-sized crowd waited for the field to make their scheduled return an estimated 20 minutes later. We waited, waited and waited until, by 11am, it became obvious something had gone wrong.

Doyle, Collins and the rest of us had got as far as Mereworth before we went wrong a couple of months beforehand, but the main field did not even make it out of Medway.

Somewhere around Dock Road a race car took a wrong turning. This was always going to happen: Medway Council had apparently passed a little-known by-law decreeing that all road users should spend at least half an hour trying to get out of Chatham Dockyards and went as far as

Cyclists using a hand gesture to warn each other of traffic islands in Dock Road.

Photograph courtesy KM Group

'Vietnam!'

to remove all signs and lighting to achieve their end. The field merely did what everyone else does when trying to get out of Chatham: got helplessly lost and ended up in Luton Arches before they realised a mistake had been made.

All hell broke loose. Most people, when confronted with the vista presented by Luton's railway bridge, want to get out as quickly as possible, but after flinging their toys from the collective pram the riders spent the best part of half an hour debating whether or not they should 'protest'.

To understand what happened next, a brief introduction is needed to the role of the 'patron' in the feudal world of professional cycling. The literal translation from the French means 'boss' and the mafia connotations are anything but accidental. The patron rules on race etiquette, deciding on everything from when the riders should take their 'natural break' to whether or not attackers should be chased down and even – in extreme cases – who should actually win.

The patron is invariably the strongest rider in the bunch and the role is passed on from generation to generation. Eddy Merckx begat Bernard Hinault, Hinault begat Greg LeMond, LeMond begat Miguel Indurain and Indurain begat Lance Armstrong.

Armstrong took the role seriously, typified by an episode in the 2004 Tour de France when Filippo Simeoni, a rider who had served a ban for doping offences and had pointed the finger at others, tried to attack on

Millar, having taken the Gillingham sprint, waits for help in Chatham.

the stage to Lons-Le-Saunier. Simeoni's group was chased down by Armstrong, who despite having the yellow jersey in the bag, was determined to deny Simeoni even the chance of a stage win.

The Guardian's William Fotheringham accurately described it as the behaviour of a playground bully, but you still needed to be a certain kind of character to play the role.

When Armstrong retired in 2005 he left a vacuum and Boonen, essentially a nice guy who lacked the Texan's steel, seemed ill-equipped for the mantle. Confronted with 77 other riders and a host of contradictory demands, Boonen made a decision that infuriated some of the riders, particularly Aylesham's Kristian House – that there would be 'no racing today'.

When the field finally ambled past Rochester Castle, Boonen was locked in conversation with Roger Hammond, arguably the most experienced British rider racing professionally at the time. It looked amicable enough, but the bitterness that lay beneath the surface became apparent just minutes after the stage finish. As soon as the race left Rochester, I jumped in the company Corsa and bombed down to Goudhurst, which I thought would be the best vantage point. Several hundred other people had had the same idea, meaning I had to park halfway into a ditch in a lane a quarter of a mile from the village centre, but any worries I had about being late were quickly banished.

Again I waited half an hour before the first ripple of applause from down the slopes could be heard. The sound built up to a polite level, but the peloton seemed to be taking it very easy and at that point nobody had any idea why.

KM photographer Andy Payton, a motorsport fanatic, was unimpressed: 'And they wonder why people are cynical about professional cycling…' he muttered as he drove off to his next job.

The BBC footage later showed DFL's directeur sportif Eric Vanderaeden urging his riders to race, while Chris Boardman, himself a victim of the cynicism of the European bunch, openly told viewers that a few of the riders fancied an easy day and were obviously not up for it.

By the time the pack got to Dover, keener observers knew something was up and the riders were greeted with abuse as well as applause. House, defying Boonen's dictat, attacked on the way out of the town towards Sixmile, but he was chased down, verbally abused and spat at by riders whose self-serving hypocrisy became apparent as soon as the finish line loomed into view.

With the carrot of a stage win and UCI ranking points dangled in front of them, the 'no racing' policy suddenly went out of the window and the club run morphed into a furious sprint, won by the Italian Francesco Chicchi, ahead of Britain's ascendant star Mark Cavendish.

Dock Road, minus cars.

The view from Blue Bell Hill on the A229 towards Maidstone.

In the Press area we still were not fully up to speed with what had happened, until a visibly upset House walked into the trailer and gave us a scoop. He clearly wanted to get everything off his chest and Steve Constable of *The Kentish Gazette* and myself were treated to a first-hand account of exactly what had gone on.

There was anger in House's eyes, mixed with disbelief. He looked like a man who was trying to come to terms with seeing his dream indelibly tarnished. This was a man who would clearly never feel the same way about bike racing ever again and I knew exactly how he felt – it was how I felt when I finished Paul Kimmage's autobiography.

House would carry on racing, of course, with significant success on the British circuit, but this was the day a part of his professional dream died.

'There were a few problems but it's going to happen in any race. It's a great course, some of the climbs are really challenging, but it wasn't fun.

'The Tour started well, but for me it lost a lot of meaning after Saturday. It was my home stage. I had my friends and family along the route and many had painted my name on the road.'

He couldn't have poured his heart out any more if he'd been sitting on a psychiatrist's couch. 'I might not get the chance again and it was taken away from me. During the race I told Boonen that it was my home stage but he just shrugged.'

As the World Champion, Boonen would have been someone House looked up to and aspired to emulate. His internal conflict spilled out as he mounted a faltering defence of the Belgian.

'In his defence he did what he said he would do and didn't race,' House said, before remembering a further act of betrayal. 'But his team did win the stage, which was kind of a kick in the teeth.'

That was some understatement. The world time-trial champion, Michael Rogers, was wheeled out to defend the go-slow.

Despite the fact that he was Australian, it was difficult to dislike Rogers.

Before the start of the stage in Rochester he should have been resting in the T-Mobile team car, but rather than put his feet up he got out to help a steward who was struggling to move one of the steel barriers.

Yet after this debacle he sounded like an apologist for the militants: 'We do understand the organisers have a difficult situation with the police and that it's not easy for them to achieve complete road closure, but we ask, fairly so, that for the safety of everyone we can have clear roads.

'We don't want to see anyone get hurt or killed and if the race goes on in this condition that could be possible.'

Nobody was going to disagree with the first sentiment, but there were ways and means of making a point without resorting to the kind of

A television cameraman goes beyond the call of duty to get a shot of the break going down Blue Bell Hill. On the opposite carriageway someone tries to keep up.

Photograph courtesy KM Group

CSC lead the charge down
Blue Bell Hill.

industrial action that could kill the sport. They could have held a sit-down protest, gone slow for a few miles or simply aimed a few barbs in the press afterwards.

More to the point, if it was too dangerous to race, why did the riders suddenly feel it was safe enough to contest the final sprint?

Later I spotted an irked-looking Doyle, though he managed a belated smile of recognition when I reminded him of the ride we had been on two months previously. He tried to put a brave face on it, saying 'It was a bonus for the people of Rochester – they had the race for 50 minutes instead of 20,' but he wasn't fooling anyone. I asked him about the no-race pact and he blamed the Italians: 'They were the ones who said they weren't going to race and then they were the ones sprinting at the end. It was just like the football World Cup.'

Doyle, a Chelsea fan, was clearly more riled than he was letting on. I wasn't sure how valid his football comparison was, though the parallels with the Pakistan cricket team's decision to refuse to play England after being accused of ball tampering seemed more obvious. Had Pakistan played on and made their point after the game, the biggest story to hit the sport's pages that summer would have been quickly forgotten, but in cricket that kind of protest was unusual.

The Caisse d'Epargne team take it easy at the back.

The bunch approaches the Medway Tunnel.

In cycling it seemed all too familiar. As a reporter I felt conflicting emotions. On the one hand, I had a great story. On the other, the story was that an event I desperately wanted to succeed had degenerated into a farce. A sport I loved had managed to score a spectacular own-goal and I was one of the men lined up to give it a kicking.

The one consolation was that there was no way these scenes would be repeated when the Tour de France came to Kent. The French didn't mess about with 'rolling' road closures that allowed cars to leak onto the route. The stewards were not going to let anyone go the wrong way and, barring a major incident (always possible in cycling), Boonen would not be called upon to preside over a kangaroo court. Whether anybody would turn out to watch after this fiasco, however, was another matter.

Chapter 8

PAT BUTCHER OR ANGELINA JOLIE?

The Tour de France, meanwhile, had problems of its own. Landis could not be stripped of his title until the protracted legal process was concluded, meaning Pereiro could not be declared the winner. The fallout from the Operation Puerto affair rumbled on and a fresh batch of riders had been discredited. The pollution of the Tour continued unabated, but by now at least ASO were determined to do something about it.

In November 2006 a delegation from Kent County Council, plus a number of journalists, were invited to Paris to witness the unveiling of the route for the 2007 Tour. It was basically a junket, but the choice of a day

Bichot's facial expression betrays the effort needed to stay in front at Medway.

Photograph courtesy KM Group

in our offices on the Medway City Estate and a day on the Eurostar and in the Palais de Congrés was like the choice between a night with Pat Butcher or Angelina Jolie.

We already knew the route, from our trip to London, but that did not mean it wasn't fascinating to watch 3,000 people cram into the auditorium.

Some of them even deserved to be there – among the clusters of hangers-on there were genuine achievers like Hinault and Pereiro. Unfortunately Virenque was also there, being treated like an A-list celebrity by his fawning coterie of apologists in the French Press. The very sight of this unctuous, preening drug cheat made me want to vomit.

Ironically the sight of me made Ken Livingstone want to vomit, though that was still some way off. First we had to sit through the Tour's promotional film. I again felt a swell of pride as the name of my hometown was mentioned, though as the route of the Kent stage was now common knowledge, I was more interested in the way the film had been edited.

Given that Lance Armstrong had dominated the previous seven races, ASO deserved some credit for producing over half an hour of material that did not once mention him by name. It was as if they had decided to

A Quick Step rider, surrounded by Bouyges Telecom rivals.

Photograph courtesy KM Group

Millar stays in the saddle at St Margaret's Street, Rochester, while his companions are forced out of the saddle.

deny his very existence, although if anyone was about to accuse them of sweeping the doping issue under the carpet, they had not yet seen what they had in store for Landis.

The American was centre stage for a resumé of the 2006 race. They showed his sweating carcass after his collapse on the road to La Toussuire, when he lost eight minutes to Pereiro and looked a broken man. He then reappeared a day later, Landis the redeemer, Landis the Messiah, Landis of the ludicrously flared nostrils, looking like a cross between Arnold Rimmer and Vitali Klitschko as he crossed the finish line at the top of the Joux Plane. They then showed him in the yellow jersey he claimed in the final time trial, wearing it in Paris, before homing in on his goofy American face, with its orange goatee beard and mildly stupid grin.

The image before us was about 10m high on the screen and just when you were thinking 'this is a bit weird, even for the French', they shattered Landis's face, sending segments of eye, nose and baseball cap in multiple directions.

It wasn't subtle, but I liked it. It said, in a none too roundabout way, that if you mess us about, we'll blow you up.

The Tour needed that. And it needed to hear what ASO's President Patrick Leclerc had to say next, when he grabbed the mic: 'I often said doping was cycling's number-one problem. I'm not pleased that I was right, but I feel that the succession of doping scandals in 2006 gives us some hope. The yellow jersey was tarnished but we have scored points in the fight against doping. Cheats will find it harder and harder to get away with it.'

It was a pity nobody had said this in 1998, 1988, 1978 or 1968, but better late than never.

Livingstone then took to the stage. This was a man who polarised public opinion more completely than any post-war politician, with the exception of Margaret Thatcher, and yet on the Eurostar journey from Ashford to Paris even the Conservative councillors in our group had been giving him qualified praise for his implementation of the congestion charge.

He said a single word in French, 'Bonjour', before addressing the hall in English.

After sitting through another over-gushing tribute to LeBlanc, when he finally got to the meat of his speech the thought did occur that we could do

Millar, about to become the first cyclist to legally ride through the Medway Tunnel.

with someone like him in Kent, a man who had a vision and someone who at least offered the electorate an alternative to the prevailing form of politics we had, where apathy was almost actively encouraged.

Most of the mud thrown by the anti-Livingstone brigade usually centred on cost. If Livingstone wanted to do something he would find a way of doing it, regardless of the financial implications.

I once spent a summer working for Maidstone Borough Council, in an era when every photocopy had to be accounted for. If you bought a vol-au-vent on expenses someone would claim you were robbing the tax-payer. For example, when the Mayor of Poitiers came to the county town to attend a so-called Festival of Europe in 1992, a council official decided the best way to introduce him to Maidstone was to put him up in a bed and breakfast in

The CSC team lead the
main field up a sharp
section of the Pilgrims
Way.

Buckland Road. Realising a diplomatic incident would break out if the mayor had his breakfast served by Maidstone's answer to the afore-mentioned Pat Butcher, a French official quickly made a reservation for the Stakis Hotel (now the Hilton at Vinters Park).

'Twinning' festivals were an excruciating embarrassment. Dignitaries from Maidstone would be treated to opulent banquets in Beauvais, but when their French counterparts returned to England they were fobbed off with a few cocktail sausages by cringing council officials, worried that if they splashed out on anything more elaborate a rent-a-gob councillor would spend the next six months bleating about it.

The upshot of these conflicting approaches was that London got to stage the Olympics and Maidstone got to stage its annual river festival, which amounted to a couple of jazz bands, a few boats, a host of shirtless ASBOs jumping off the old bridge and some fireworks.

The damage done to the town's image by this thriftiness can only be guessed at. It was amazing that the Tour was actually coming through Maidstone at all, as it had successfully bypassed Kent's capital in 1994.

As tempting as it was to get mullered on the gallons of top-quality booze swilling around the Palais, I still had a job to do and when I spotted that Bradley Wiggins had been left unattended for a few seconds I asked him for a quick interview.

Augé leads the break on the Pilgrims Way between Borstal and Burham.

Photograph courtesy KM Group

Photograph courtesy Alan Constable

Wiggins, his hair dragged into a style that aped his idol Paul Weller, was used to suffering idiots and he would have been asked almost everything a thousand times before. The national, non-specialist journos always seemed to ask 'Can you do it?'

'Bradley, can you win the prologue?'

'Roger/Rafa/Andy do you think Tim Henman can win Wimbledon?'

'Sir Alex, do you think you can beat Exeter in the replay?'

It was an idiotic way of asking a question, because if the answer was negative it would defeat the very object of the exercise, though it seems to be on page one of the Sky Sports training manual.

Regional hacks just wanted the local angle and were looking for a link, no matter how dubious, with their patch. Wiggins, to my eternal gratitude, was polite and went through the motions with me.

Yes, he had ridden in Kent before, in criteriums held in Ashford and Canterbury city centres, and he said he was planning a reconnaissance mission that winter, 'I will probably check out the Kent stage in December or January. We'll definitely do one day in Kent – I don't think any of the other teams will be checking it out.'

Kuchynski (far left) and Grivko share a joke as they climb the A229 into Maidstone, near the Running Horse roundabout.

Prudhomme had been almost casually dismissive of the stage during the presentation, considering it 'A generally flat stage that favours the sprinters.'

Wiggins did not disagree. As a Londoner his priority was Saturday's prologue, though he did not discount the prospect of a stage win altogether. 'I think it's really a stage for the sprinters,' he admitted, though, perhaps sensing this wasn't what I wanted to hear, he added, 'but you never know. Someone might be able to get away in the final kilometres.'

Continental riders did sometimes get caught out by the unexpected severity of British hills, but with a 10-mile plateau and descent after the final climb at Farthing Corner, Wiggins was not going to insult anyone's intelligence.

'When you're riding up the Col Du Galibier and riding for an hour and 20 minutes it doesn't really compare,' he said, which at least gave me the chance to ask him a different kind of question. In everything I had read about cycling, the overwhelming theme was suffering. Was it still possible to enjoy the Tour when you were in the second hour of an Alpine climb?

'Yeah,' he said, as if aware that cyclists had a tendency to moan and this might be a useful opportunity to redress that.

But before he could finish he was dragged away.

Livingstone was standing there, looking at me as if I'd just slipped poison in his whisky. The mayor could not see beyond my notepad. To him I was a reporter and reporters were made of something he wouldn't even tread in. Given the treatment he received at the hands of Associated Newspapers I could understand that, especially as the Palais de Congrés junket took place in the aftermath of the row sparked by the throwaway remark he made about *Daily Mail* journalists being like concentration camp guards.

He looked at me in such a way I thought he might actually vomit on my shoes and then whisked Wiggins away for a private audience, but I didn't take it personally. I had got my interview in the bag and now it was time to uphold the finest traditions of the profession by hitting the bar, as any self-respecting journalist would on finding himself in a foreign capital.

Chapter 9

HERO

As the race day drew nearer, the sport continued to tie itself in knots. The Italians could always be relied on to generate a scandal and, with depressing predictability, the nation that gave us Pantani and Basso managed to destroy the credibility of the 2007 Giro d'Italia before a cleat had clipped into a pedal. Home favourite Danilo Di Luca was allowed to ride despite his ongoing involvement in a 'drugs for oil' scandal, which dated back to 2004.

Suspicion clung to Di Luca like porridge to a spoon, but the organisers of the Giro looked the other way and Di Luca subsequently destroyed the field, routing his rivals to win the pink jersey and in the process chalking up yet another victory that only the most credulous of Italian fans could have 100 per cent faith in. When Di Luca was subsequently found to have

The bunch on the northern entrance to Maidstone.

Jens Vogt leads the field into Maidstone, with a spectacular show of strength at the front.

raced with 'abnormally' low levels of hormone on a key stage to Monte Zoncolan it was head-slappingly frustrating, though at least this time the Press had seen it coming.

The year of Basso's thrilling, stylish victory in 2006 was followed by so crushing a fall from grace that when we watched Di Luca 12 months later the question was when, not if, the scandal would break. Yet watching the race on Eurosport it was obvious that the Tifosi, the term given to Italian fans, wouldn't have cared if Di Luca had hopped on a motorbike. Roadside banners fêted him alongside Pantani and Basso, champions in a land where idols were believed incapable of any transgression. The idea that Di Luca was a cheat was impossible for many Italians to accept, so they chose to aggressively deny his failings and those of the other dopers.

In Italy this worked. In Britain it was not going to wash. The idea that British sportsmen had always aspired to a Corinthian ideal, placing honour ahead of victory, was a myth, but enough of the ethos had survived into the 21st century to make sure that drugged athletes were never going to be cut the kind of slack in the UK that they were afforded in Italy or Spain.

We needed a British hero and David Millar, despite his very British *mea culpa* on his use of EPO, represented damaged goods for some, particularly Paul Kimmage, who advocated a life ban.

Bradley Wiggins was more like it and as a potential stage winner his star rose as the race approached, but there was another Briton who was about to tackle the Tour and who was an even better symbol of the things that made one proud to be British – the former Crystal Palace and England footballer Geoff Thomas.

For football supporters of a certain generation, the idea that the word 'hero' would ever be applied to Thomas strained credulity. He typified the Graham Taylor era, when the optimism generated by Italia '90 withered and died. One moment above all summed up the limitations of the English game, when England played France at Wembley in 1992. With England winning 1–0, Thomas played a one-two with Gary Lineker and found himself through on goal, with only the French 'keeper Gilles Rousset to beat. As Rousset rushed off his line, Thomas decided to be clever and attempted to lob him from around 45 yards. Instead, his shot nearly hit the corner flag and his career entered a tailspin. Thomas was, in reality, a box-to-box midfielder, whose sheer drive and energy made up for his technical limitations. He had a highly respectable career at Palace, Wolves and Nottingham Forest, but the poverty of talent available to England at the time thrust him into a role he wasn't up to and his chip against France ensured he would captain many people's All-Time England

The bunch on Maidstone bridge.

Photograph courtesy KM Group

Worst XI. But to put that into perspective, had Thomas been born in Kent, he would have been one of the county's most celebrated players.

Thomas's chip earned him a level of infamy. Comedians David Baddiel and Rob Newman performed a sketch likening it to the moment Kennedy was shot in Dallas and suggesting it was a global conspiracy to ensure Thomas never again got near an England team ('Who benefits? Everybody.')

It would have been a dismal way to be remembered, but Thomas's story was about to take a more serious turn. A couple of years into his retirement, he was holidaying in Majorca when he doubled up in agony on the tennis court. He ignored increasingly serious symptoms for over a month before finally agreeing to visit a doctor, whose diagnosis made Thomas's nightmare at Wembley seem trivial.

At the age of 39 he discovered that he had leukaemia and his chances of surviving more than three years hinged on finding a successful bone marrow donor. Like Lance Armstrong, Thomas was told the odds on him surviving were effectively less than 50 per cent, but when his sister proved a viable donor he was handed the chance to live. Yet like Armstrong, Thomas was haunted by the memory of cancer sufferers he befriended and who did not make it through.

The bunch on Maidstone bridge.

Photograph courtesy KM Group

The CSC team leads the bunch as it ambles up Maidstone's Tonbridge Road.

Having beaten the disease, nobody would have thought any less of Thomas if he had decided to spend the rest of his days gardening, but having read Armstrong's autobiography he decided to ride the route of the 2004 Tour de France, in the face of expert advice from people whose only interest was in preventing him from doing his health serious damage.

Astonishingly he pulled it off, though his book, *Riding Through the Storm*, contains several X-rated passages as he recounts how he struggled to pedal at 6mph through the mountains and ended up doing a hundred miles more than the professionals due to the dubious map-reading skills of his support staff. Nonetheless, he finished and this feat alone, for me, puts Thomas above every other footballer England has ever produced in terms of his achievements.

Three years later he clearly felt the need to put his body through another ordeal in the name of charity and a 25-strong party of journalists, PR agents and BCF officials accompanied him on a two-stage media ride through Kent, to drum up publicity for his second Tour de France, in which he would spend eight days riding alongside his old Palace teammate Ian Wright.

Some sports stars have questionable motives behind their charity work, seeing personal appearances as little more than PR opportunities and, in some cases, a chance to line their already vast pockets. Thomas looked

Nobody knew who this man was, but they'll cheer anything in the county town, as the author discovered when he waved a Maidstone United scarf out of his car window.

Photograph courtesy KM Group

upon the business of saving other people's lives as a full-time job. His time was entirely devoted to training and satisfying media commitments, and this meant that in every interview he produced the same well-rehearsed answers. If he tired of doing them he did not let on when I spoke to him, a couple of days after the ride.

Grabbing him for a chat in a bunch of 25 riders proved impossible. I stayed with him for the 50 miles between Rochester and Goudhurst and one of his teammates, a fellow cancer survivor, urged me to join them on the second half of the stage to Canterbury, but the memories of clinging to Doyle's back wheel a year beforehand were still fresh.

By stopping at the Star & Eagle, I managed to enjoy the ride while reinforcing my respect for the guys who were accompanying Thomas on his second Tour.

I rang him later that week for a proper interview.

'Other blood cancer sufferers weren't as lucky as me,' he said. 'They need new state-of-the-art drugs to save their lives and that's where the Geoff Thomas Foundation is trying to help.

'The UK is the world leader in medical research and our aim is to fund blood cancer nurses who will help get new drugs from the scientist's lab bench to the patient's hospital bedside.'

He did not tell me anything he had not already told 100 other reporters – what else was he going to say? But by publicising his efforts we at least gave people another connection to the Tour de France and a way of seeing it as a supreme physical challenge.

Chapter 10

CONTENDERS

D rumming up enthusiasm for the actual participants wasn't as easy. With Lance gone and no Landis to pelt with rotten fruit, the favourite was the Kazakh rider Alexandre Vinokourov, as I wrote in my first online Tour diary.

To this day I have no idea if more than a handful of people read it:

'Cycling fans anticipating the start of the 2007 Tour de France might care to draw up a bingo card of this year's fancied riders and tick off those who fall by the wayside in the two months leading up to the race.

'Trying to predict a winner at the moment is about as easy as attempting to ride a fixed-wheel bike up Boxley Hill, but by a process of elimination we can at least remove a few suspects from our enquiries.

Le peloton turns across the Medway and on to the Broadway.

Photograph courtesy Hilary Yorke

'It won't, for example, be American Floyd Landis, the "winner" of the 2006 race, whose subsequent positive drug test for testosterone shattered a sport already reeling from Operation Puerto, the Spanish drug investigation that decimated the field just days before the start of last year's race. Puerto implicated over 50 riders in a blood-doping scandal and its highest-profile casualties were the Italian Ivan Basso and Germany's Jan Ullrich.

Maidstone High Street, transformed by the absence of motor vehicles.

A staggering number of people watch on as the bunch cross the old bridge in Maidstone town centre.

'Basso, seen by many as the natural successor to Lance Armstrong, had just romped to victory in the Tour of Italy when he was linked to the breaking scandal and booted out of the race before he could turn a pedal in anger.

'Last week he made a bizarre confession, denying he had ever been doped, but claiming:

"I have not done anything illegal. It was a moment of weakness on my part. I've never taken any doping substance or undergone any illegal transfusions."

'Seemingly unaware he was contradicting himself, Basso went on to say: "I did admit having attempted to use doping for the [2006] Tour de France and I am ready to pay the penalty for that.

"All my wins have been achieved in a proper and clean manner and I have every intention of returning to action and continuing with the job I love once I have paid the penalty."

'Let's not bank on him returning anytime soon, although his chances are at least better than Ullrich's, who used the more familiar script deployed by riders when they've been caught red-handed, saying: "I never once cheated as a cyclist." When Ullrich won the 1997 Tour at the age of just 23 he was poised to dominate the sport for a decade, but instead of training he appeared to develop an addiction to pies. His career was derailed by a weight problem, recreational drugs (with startling originality he claimed his drink was spiked with speed) and finally Puerto.

'He denied any wrongdoing, but his retirement appeared to be a pre-emptive strike, particularly when his DNA sample matched a bag of blood seized by the Spanish authorities, leaving him looking as guilty as a puppy sitting next to a pile.

'So who's left? Last year's moral victor was the second-placed Oscar Pereiro, but he owed his success (still not ratified by Tour organisers) to a freak breakaway on the 13th stage, taking over 28 minutes on his rivals, enough for him to cling to the runners'-up slot in Paris. Having caught the field napping once, this year he'll be a man marked by stronger riders, including German Andreas Kloden, third last year and the Spaniard Alejandro Valverde, arguably the sport's most promising all-rounder.

'Pitched out of the 2006 race by a broken collar bone, Valverde will be a favourite this time round if he steers clear of injury and scandal, as will the Italian Damiano Cunego, provided he doesn't dip into his reserves too deeply during the Tour of Italy.

'For a wild card keep an eye on the manic Alexandre Vinokourov, the most gloriously unhinged member of the peloton.

The surreal sight of a giant lion, with its thumbs aloft, in central Maidstone, part of the Tour's publicity 'caravan'.

Photograph courtesy KCC

Photograph courtesy KM Group

The procession of team vehicles follows their riders across the Fairmeadow bridge onto the Broadway bearing spare bicycles.

"Vino", Kazakhstan's second most famous export, is the sport's current showman, attacking relentlessly and riding with a grimace that makes him look like something trying to sink his teeth into Sigourney Weaver. Robbed of the chance to compete last year when his team was booted out in the aftermath of the Puerto affair, Vino, who wasn't implicated in the scandal, proved a point by going on to win the Tour of Spain. At 33 he may not have time on his side, but he'll either win or fail gloriously.

'Only two British riders are likely to start in London. Time-trial specialist David Millar is the better bet for the overall standings, but has had a quiet spring. Olympic gold medallist Bradley Wiggins may be timing his run to perfection, having just won the prologue to the Four Days of Dunkirk. Wiggins once used to race round the streets of Ashford as a junior – if he fulfills his potential and wins the Tour Prologue in London, he'll return to Kent with the yellow jersey on his shoulders.'

Rather skilfully I managed to avoid picking a single winner. Five British riders made it to the start line instead of the predicted two, but I did at least get the bingo card scenario right.

Chapter 11

NO PARKING

In the weeks leading up to the race physical evidence of the impending arrival of the Tour began to surface as yellow 'no parking' signs lined the route.

Amanda Lumley, as Kent County Council's Tour de France co-ordinator, was charged with the logistical operation of making sure everyone knew what was about to hit them.

'We did a series of "roadshows" for parishes very early on and tried to engage with as many groups as possible to explain about the event, the road closures and also the opportunities to hold events on the day,' she said. 'The other partners, including Kent police, NHS, Fire and many other community services including, of course, the media, who were also

Kuchynski waves to the crowd on Maidstone bridge.

Photograph courtesy KM Group

David Millar takes
instructions from his
team car as the break
climbs the Tonbridge Road
in Maidstone.

involved very early on, gave consistent messages to try to ensure as many people as possible knew about the event.'

Yet the sheer scale of the job meant major difficulties were inevitable.

'We had to communicate to people throughout the route that the roads would be closed and plan contingencies for approximately 100,000 homes that were cut off by road closures,' she said. 'Generally when we explained about the Tour most people were very welcoming and excited about it.'

Not everyone shared the enthusiasm though. The local media began to carry sob stories from locals who would be 'prisoners in their own homes' on the day of the race – a description which conjured up the image of armed gendarmes pointing assault rifles at innocent civilians wanting to leave their driveways.

Photograph courtesy KM Group

Three-year-old Joshua Brundish, sporting a teddy on his handlebars.

One usually sensible website ran the following introduction: 'Residents could be trapped in their homes by the Tour de France because they do not know the extent to which roads will be closed for the event, a council fears.

'Dartford Borough Council is worried many people have not received details from the county council about the cycling race, which arrives in Kent on Sunday 8 July. More than 10,000 households in the borough will be affected by road closures.

'Cllr Patsy Thurlow, Dartford council's portfolio holder for leisure, said: "I'm sure lots of people think the roads will only close for a few minutes, but it will be at least three hours and more likely four or five.

'"I'm sure that the organisers have a lot to do but we are concerned that many local people simply don't know what the road closures will mean to them and we are not very happy about this situation."'

In some cases their fears were legitimate. The English public transport infrastructure being what it is, some people were presented with major logistical headaches getting to work.

These included Matt Davison, who was supposed to be orchestrating BBC Radio Kent's coverage from their studios in Tunbridge Wells and realised he wouldn't be able to drive there from his home in Gravesend.

'I found out my road was going to shut at 8am, so I overcompensated and stayed somewhere overnight,' he said.

I was in a similar boat – my house in Fant was cut off from the motorway network by the closure to the Tonbridge Road, though had I actually needed to I could simply have parked a couple of hundred metres away and crossed the road on foot.

And there was also an element of Clarkson-esque whining about the episode, with salad-dodging motorists unable to accept that for one day only they'd be unable to drive the 400 yards down the road to their local Lidl, when God knows some of them could have done with the exercise.

If you really want to depress yourself about the state of the county's gene pool, simply tune in to a local radio phone-in, or better still a 'web chat' and wait for your view of humanity to plunge as you plough through the semi-literate ramblings of fellow citizens. The bastion of enlightened thinking that is the *News Shopper Online* carried a remark from Anon of Dartford: 'Excited by the Tour? Like hell we are! Trapped and frustrated.'

Barming residents, armed with folding chairs, await the race.

Photograph courtesy John Kavanagh

KW of Strood dipped into a well of purer bigotry: 'Why the hell has Tour de France, have to come here [sic]. When 500 people took to the route last sunday, no roads were closed, no traffic diverted, no hassle. Two hundred people want to do it and its carnage. STAY IN FRANCE.'

That, however, is the great thing about freedom of speech. Everyone has the right to their opinion, no matter how intellectually stunted it makes them look and everyone has the right to tell them, in reply, that they are talking out of their most southerly orifice.

To wit one resident of Herts, who took the time to reply: 'What a pathetic, tiny-minded attitude! One of the world's greatest sporting spectacles comes through your rather unspectacular little town and you are whingeing? You should be grateful that, if only for a few minutes, Dartford will be on television around the world. It's the only way anybody outside South London will ever hear of it (except for some fellow called Jagger, of course). I expect you're upset because you can't get into your car for an hour or two. Well, how sad. Try walking for a change.'

There were other, more pleasant precursors to the race. As the sports editor of a local newspaper I was perceived as influential by PR people, who regularly rang me up at the worst possible moments and then rang me back to check I had received their press release and to ask if I would be using it.

Eventual race winner Alberto Contador follows George Hincapie (obscured) while the soon-to-be-disgraced Alexandre Vinokourov (right, bright green glasses) chats with a teammate as the bunch passes the Glebe Lane junction in Barming.

The Sussex Beef Society
sussexcattle@btinternet.com

Cyclists
for Speed, Strength
& Stamina

Eat **Sussex** Beef

The Great British Beef Breed

Photograph courtesy KM Group

A farmer's advertising board for Sussex beef makes claims that might raise eyebrows among nutritionists.

In the month leading up to the Tour the usual offers to attend tedious luncheons at local golf courses were replaced by offers of agreeable freebies – a French language version of *Treasures of the Tour de France*, offers to watch the race at specially selected venues (all of which I had to decline) and a complimentary copy of *Blazing Saddles* by Matt Rendell, along with the chance to meet the author at a book signing in the Maidstone branch of Waterstones.

Having read all Rendell's books on cycling I happily accepted the chance to meet him on the Tuesday before the race. Rendell falls into the category of people who love cycling more than I ever will. A tall, slightly gangling, bespectacled man in his early 40s, Rendell, who hails from Wilmington near Dartford, had, like Armstrong and Thomas, survived a form of cancer and retained an infectious enthusiasm for his sport. Yet in his case his love of cycling survived not only a brush with terminal illness, but also the fall-out from his iconoclastic biography of the disgraced former Tour 'winner' Marco Pantani, the late Italian cyclist who died in 2004 from a cocaine overdose.

Rendell's research uncovered the sheer scale of Pantani's treachery and it was impossible to read his work without having any illusions you clung to about the sport's integrity shattered.

There was compelling evidence that Pantani used EPO and growth hormone dating back to 1992. Even if the bulk of the peloton was doing likewise, it could not excuse the individual's transgressions, which Rendell documented meticulously, including the time an injured Pantani's advisers tried to whisk him away from doctors who were trying to treat him after a near-fatal crash so that he could be tended to by his 'private' medical staff, and the time he finally fell foul of the testers when he was poised to win the 1999 Giro d'Italia. As ever, by writing about these crimes Rendell was regarded in Italy as a far bigger criminal than the man who actually committed them.

The peloton at Wateringbury.

Yet as we talked about the Tour in the coffee lounge Rendell managed to remain relentlessly upbeat. His mood darkened only once, when he recalled a trip he made to Italy to attend a conference, after publishing his exposé.

'Pantani's parents were there…I was frightened of a lynching, so I just shut up. Italy is fanatical about sport in a way that's a notch above Britain, but it also has the most competent anti-doping agencies. They were Marco's best friends because they were the only people trying to save his life.'

He suffered nocturnal panic attacks and nightmares while writing the book and was subjected to death threats after its conclusion. For someone who was ostensibly trying to flog his latest book, a history of the Tour de France, Rendell was agreeably unwilling to spout the usual, vacuous PR line when talking about the race.

'The Tour de France defies the laws of physics,' he said. 'It shouldn't exist it's so discredited, but it's such a great story. This is the death of Tom Simpson times 10 – it could be the first time a global sport dies on its feet, although the French government won't let it die because it's a massive publicity video for the French tourist board.'

He was equally scathing about Floyd Landis, whom he described as 'a despicable man.' He expanded at length, his only really printable observation being: 'He comes across as a kind of goofy, gonzo cyclist, suffering from cross-cultural dislocation.'

Rendell then offered a convincing explanation for the Tour's enduring popularity. 'The Tour is coming to Britain and you don't need to understand it to get a lot out of it. Tennis is two people hitting a ball back to each other and cricket is incomprehensible, but you can look at this brightly coloured peloton going past and say, "I don't know what's going on, but it's great."'

And with that, conscious of the 30 or so people waiting to grill him about the Tour in the coffee shop behind us, we wrapped up the interview, with me somewhat naïvely saying that I hoped I would bump into him in London, still unaware that in a media village of that size I was more likely to bump into Tom Simpson.

Chapter 12

THE FRENCH. AGAIN.

O n the Friday before the race, I decided to squeeze in a quick mountain-bike ride before heading into London to collect my accreditation.

Riding through Barming Woods, my phone rang. It was *The Kent Messenger*'s Andy Rayfield, telling me our Ford Focus had not been fitted with an official race radio and that someone, probably me, was going to have to drive up to Docklands to get it fixed.

As Londoners are biologically incapable of driving motor vehicles I found this prospect about as enticing as the idea of a candlelit dinner with Carol Thatcher, but an hour later Rayfield rang back to say our driver, Ron Keeble, was taking the motor and I could head in on the train.

It took nearly two hours to get from Barming to Excel, a cavernous exhibition centre in London's Docklands that it can take 10 minutes to walk through.

The experience was a wholly unwanted trip down memory lane, as I renewed acquaintances with the many faces of French bureaucracy.

Without a pass at the Tour de France, you may as well be a stalker trying to scale the gates of a celebrity mansion and we were told passes would only be handed to accredited media with photo ID.

When I presented the relevant ID to the teenager behind the press counter he went to a cardboard box, rifled through it and came back with nothing.

Teston, which hosted the second sprint, was the scene of a fatal road accident months before the race, prompting a campaign for safer roads through the village.

Photograph courtesy KM Group

89

'Your colleague collect eet,' he shrugged.

How could I have forgotten? In France an act as simple as borrowing a library book requires you to fill in a form and come back an hour later in the hope that a librarian has found it on the shelves you could have browsed yourself. So why should I have expected my pass to be anywhere else than the clutches of a 'colleague'?

After half a dozen phone calls I went back to this French equivalent of a Harry Enfield teenager and asked him, politely, if he wouldn't mind having another look. He promptly delved into another box and produced the magic, laminated pass within seconds. Had he been switched on an extra half an hour of anxiety would have been avoided, but that would be missing the point. Industrial action, pointless bureaucracy and general misanthropy of front desk staff are something to be cherished when dealing with the French – who'd want to deal with the Germans, with their politeness, general efficiency and ability to get things done?

Had I not wasted this half an hour, I might have been more up to speed on the storm that was brewing elsewhere in the building. Eight French and German team directors, in a desperate attempt to preserve the race's credibility, withdrew from their union, claiming they could no longer associate themselves with their colleagues. Drugs, as always, were the reason for the row, with six team managers refusing to adhere to the body's ethical code.

The six teams in question all intended to field riders implicated in the Operation Puerto drug scandal, despite the sport's governing body, the UCI, insisting that any rider starting the Tour must sign a declaration stating they would ride cleanly.

Patrick Lefevre, of the Quick Step team, acted as the chief apologist, telling reporters: 'I am neither God, nor a judge and I cannot exclude anybody because of what the Press have said, or rumours.

'If a national federation gives me a name I can act, but if the Spanish

Billiards on Wateringbury Rec.

The A228, for once free of juggernauts.

Judiciary says the dossier [from Operation Puerto] cannot be used, my hands and feet are tied.'

This convenient abdication of responsibility sparked a walk-out by Roger Legeay, the vice-president of the union and once Chris Boardman's coach, who said 'You must have credible riders in front of you. We must show that we are applying our code.'

The AG2R team were one of the eight to quit the union, with their manager Vincent Lavenu claiming that some rival managers had signed the UCI declaration with 'a pistol to their temple'.

The French sports daily, *L'Equipe*, diagnosed the Tour as suffering from '*L'Equipe* remained required reading for anyone covering the Tour, but the hypocrisy of its editors was at its most absurdly transparent that day, when it ran an article claiming it had 'irrefutable' proof that Lance Armstrong had used EPO in 1999. The allegations, first made in 2005, were anything but irrefutable and Armstrong had to spend thousands of dollars defending his reputation.

Photograph courtesy Diane Fryd

Kent Police kept race-side incidents to a minimum.

The staff at *L'Equipe* were still openly wrestling with their inner demons, as was Amanda Lumley, the Kent County Council's Tour co-ordinator, who, 35 miles away in deepest Kent, was having her own mild internal crisis. 'I remember something which really stuck in my mind about two days before the race on the Friday morning,' she recalled. 'I was driving down the M20 and just before junction 6, as I turned off into Maidstone, I saw one of the matrix signs lit up with the words "Tour de France 8 July expect delays".

'At that point I suddenly felt quite sick and the reality that it was all about to happen suddenly hit me like a brick. It was rather like being at the top of the hill on a rollercoaster ride and looking down with the fear, excitement and anticipation all thrown into one.'

Lumley's feelings seemed typical of anyone who was involved with the race in a professional capacity.

On the Saturday of the prologue in London my phone rang almost constantly, with overwrought photographers and bewildered radio presenters trying to contact me, all of whom were labouring under the mistaken belief that I might have some leverage with ASO.

At that point I was simply one of thousands of punters struggling to get some kind of vantage point of the prologue course, eventually settling on a perch in Hyde Park that offered a view of about 10 metres of the road.

The official estimate suggested two million people were watching. That seemed unlikely, because it would have meant 50 people were standing by every metre of the route, but a million was a plausible figure.

If the train in from Barming had been less packed than the average commuter wagon, the city itself was definitely heaving with a different kind of tourist – from the Belgian family in their Tom Boonen T-shirts, to the bearded club enthusiasts foregoing their Saturday club runs for the chance to see the Tour.

Yet a prologue time trial is, like any time trial, an event that has more athletic merit than aesthetic appeal.

The fundamental problem with covering the stage was the sheer dullness of time-trialling as a spectator sport. Seeing one rider fly past you, albeit at high speed, simply does not have the same visual impact as watching a performer like Dennis Bergkamp or Brian Lara.

I watched the training laps. There was a ripple of applause for Bradley Wiggins and a few yells of 'Come on Brad!', but as a spectacle it was more

The bunch at Capel.

remarkable for the sheer numbers of people by the road, rather than anything the performers were doing on it. I saw the first two riders flash past, then lugged my laptop to Knightsbridge and took a tube to Green Park, where another long, frustrating walk past mile upon mile of trailers and television cabling got me to the Press area.

Most of the print hacks had remained at the media centre at Excel and only a smattering of die-hards and television reporters had congregated in our marquee, which boasted a handful of widescreen televisions but no furniture (I filed a report by sitting on the tarmac on the Mall, hunched over a laptop that was positioned on the floor in front of me).

ITV's Ned Boulting paraded up and down the finish area hunting for prey, while his Russian counterparts pleaded in vain to get Vladimir Karpets to stop for a few words as he bolted past. Some people envied the TV guys, but I didn't. It was a job that involved hours of travelling and waiting to grab a few seconds of platitudes from the protagonists. If I envied anyone in the journalistic peloton it was William Fotheringham of

The bunch at Capel.

Photograph courtesy Diane Fryd

Photograph courtesy Diane Fryd

French television cameras follow Credit Agricole rider Anthony Charteau and Bouyges Telecom's Thomas Voeckler at Capel.

The Guardian, who had the contacts and knowledge to produce some of the best Tour writing available in the English language. His relationship with David Millar allowed him to get the exclusive when he confessed to using EPO. Now he breezed into the marquee just as Millar was about to take his run at the prologue.

'Here's Dave!' he grinned as everyone waited to see if the reformed, Maltese-born, Hong Kong-raised, Aylesbury-educated Scot would complete his rehabilitation by winning the yellow jersey.

When Millar won the 2000 Tour prologue, beating Armstrong in the process, it looked like the Great British successor to Boardman had arrived. He was charismatic, articulate and hugely talented, but like too many others before him, he cracked under the pressure to deliver results. In 2003 Jeremy Whittle reported that he had become 'paranoid and defensive'. Though he won the World Time Trial Championship that year, he was living a lie and he knew it. Days before the start of the 2004 Tour he was arrested by the French police. He confessed to using EPO, but unlike the vast majority of his contemporaries he at least showed genuine contrition and it was impossible to read *L'Equipe*'s coverage of his court case without feeling moved by the way he disintegrated inside (impossible for everyone other than Paul Kimmage, that is).

The yellow jersey, Fabian Cancellara, at Capel, led by his teammates Kurt-Asle Aruesen (middle) and Christian Vande Velde.

A self-loathing Millar was handed a two-year ban. He contemplated quitting, but was coaxed back into the sport by Armstrong, among others, and decided to act as an anti-drug ambassador. Kimmage found this stance risible, but a clear majority of fans were happy to see Millar take his shot at redemption. Unfortunately for them, as Fotheringham later revealed, the Scot was in no mental state to compete.

'I have never spent so long feeling so horrible,' Millar told him. 'I'm a little nervous, a lot nervous. What feels different is my confidence. I'm riddled with self-doubt. I've no doubt about the abyss I'm going into. On a psychological level the last couple of months could have been a lot easier.'

An overawed Millar came 13th and the British sense of disappointment was compounded when Bradley Wiggins also fell short of the mark, coming a few decimal points behind third-placed George Hincapie and a massive 23 seconds behind the winner, Switzerland's Fabian Cancellara.

Wiggins's performance was hardly disgraceful, set against an astonishing display of power from Cancellara, but after seeing both Millar and Boardman win prologues in the previous decade it was difficult not to be a little disappointed, as he himself hinted in his *Guardian* column.

'Even seasoned guys in the team are saying this was one of the best Tour de France Grand Départs they have ever been to, and I'm just satisfied with the ride I did,' he wrote. 'If I had lost by one second I might have wondered if there was something else I could have done, but Fabian Cancellara was in a class of his own.'

There had been polite rather than raucous noise at 3pm when the first rider, Italy's Enrico Degano, was the first rider round the 7.9km course along Whitehall, through Hyde Park and back along the Mall.

When Wiggins set off nearly three hours later the atmosphere was incendiary.

'It was an amazing crowd, a wall of sound,' he said. 'I said beforehand that I wouldn't let it get to me but, in the end, it helped me, because I wanted to do all those people proud. It was a fantastic experience for someone like me, coming from just up the road. I'm proud to be part of it.'

Coming fourth, moreover, meant he achieved his personal minimum.

'I said if I could get in the first five that would mean I was there or thereabouts, in the ball park, I hadn't disgraced myself and there could be no reproaches.

'There was no more I could have done yesterday. I took every corner perfectly and never touched the brakes once. If I had lost by half a second, I wouldn't have been able to look back and think "Jeez. I lost it there".'

Having given everything, Wiggins was a rank outsider for Sunday, but home fans still had high hopes for Mark Cavendish and, as they were to find out, Millar had far more left in the tank.

Chapter 13

CLARET AT 8.30am

Getting to Sunday's start village at Whitehall from Maidstone required a 6am start and the 7.16 train from Maidstone West to Paddock Wood with KmFm reporter Toby Gilles and then the 'Express' to Charing Cross.

There was no margin for error, so I only began to calm down when the latter train turned up and I was able to turn my phone off for an hour.

My laminated plastic pass granted me access to the village, an incongruous set of steel fences erected in the middle of Horse Guards Parade that separated the hoi polloi from the great figures of world cycling – and Richard Virenque, the polka-dotted Cristiano Ronaldo.

Virenque's presence aside, passing through this portal was like leaving behind a world of permanent stress and entering a promised land, where

The Tonbridge Road, Maidstone, near the Lotus House takeaway early on Sunday 8 July – a normally congested stretch of the A26, absolutely devoid of cars.

Photograph courtesy Mike Flynn/Jamie Webb

Some fans used gate posts to get decent vantage points. Others used them as improvised beer tables.

it was socially acceptable to drink claret at 8.30 in the morning and stuff your face with delicacies from the complimentary patisserie counters.

We met up with our colleague Paul Hobson in an area baked in sunshine and it was already warm enough to walk around in shirt sleeves, something that promised to get the crowds out on the streets. A quick snifter of red wine had a remarkable effect and fortified me for my next task, informing ASO that I would not be able to ride shotgun on one of their motorbikes. There are people who would have regarded this as the opportunity of a lifetime, but as far as I was concerned it was the opportunity to end a lifetime. Motorcyclists to me were genocidal maniacs, for whom the highway code was a trifling obstruction to their mission to destroy all other road users. I didn't care if they wanted to purée themselves against brick walls or bounce off central reservation barriers as if they were snooker balls pinging off a cushion, but there was no way I was going to cling on to the back of one of these idiot-chauffeured machines in the name of journalism.

Thankfully the gods of health and safety came to my rescue, when the company pointed out that I was not insured for this kind of activity and I would have to cancel.

Photograph courtesy Mike Flynn/Jamie Webb

A fan tries to pick a winner.

My pleasure. Approximately 600 attempts at contacting our liaison with ASO via telephone failed, so I had to break the news to him in person when he gave us a five-minute audience in the start village.

'Ah…but deed you reeeng us?'

'Yes – approximately 600 times.'

'And you are not eeenshurred?'

'I'm afraid not. I'm sorry.'

But the relief that I was vainly trying to mask with a slightly simple grin proved slightly premature, as I found out within the hour.

The three of us ambled to our rendezvous on Northumberland Avenue, pausing to laugh at the gendarmes in their ludicrous uniforms, absurdly homo-erotic trousers that rode up into every conceivable crevice.

We were helped over the crash barriers by none other than Charly Mottet, who seemed pleasantly surprised to be recognised, even if we didn't have time to grill him on the race, and two dozen or so cars down the convoy we met our driver, Ron Keeble, leaning against a company Ford Focus.

At a guess he was in his late 50s or early 60s, but he had the lean and healthily orange look of someone who had spent his first six decades looking after himself and was thus probably fitter than a high percentage of men half his age or younger – including myself, Hobson and Gilles.

We moved off at around 10am, but at this point everything concerning the race itself became vague.

In a race vehicle, or to be more accurate in our race vehicle, the only sources of information about the stage are the naked eye, which was next to useless given we were one in a thousand vehicles in the convoy, and Radio Tour, which, though reliable, was no substitute for having a laptop and a widescreen TV.

The upshot of this was that we were far less informed about what was going on than the people we were supposed to be reporting to. For example, anyone watching at home on television or following the race on the internet would have understood why we kept stopping and starting, but we did not have a clue.

Contrary to the information published in some 'official' race guides, there was more than one start. Not only was there a ceremonial departure from Trafalgar Square, but there was also a second, ritual send-off and photo-opportunity at Tower Bridge, after a procession through central London.

Traversing this no man's land I attempted to make small talk with Keeble, who told us he 'used to do a bit of cycling.'

His name did ring a vague bell, so I asked if he had ever ridden professionally.

'Yeah, I won an Olympic medal and a few world titles,' he dead-panned, as the rest of us stifled the urge to cough out the word 'Bullsh*t!'

From Trafalgar Square to Tower Bridge the crowds were at least three deep, though how anyone arrived at the prediction there would be over a million people by the roadside I found difficult to grasp.

Keeble enlightened us. 'It's easy,' he said. 'You just count the number of legs and divide by two.'

By the time we reached Bermondsey I had grown suspicious about Keeble's cycling knowledge. The names he dropped were all well-connected and he even did a passable imitation of the UCI chairman Pat McQuaid, if by passable one means, 'sounded vaguely Irish.'

Thousands watch the bunch descend Tonbridge High Street, ahead of the first official climb of the day, Quarry Hill.

Photograph courtesy David Hodgkinson, www.sweetmoon.co.uk

I suspected, correctly, that he had successfully duped us into not believing he was an Olympian for his own personal amusement, and he eventually came clean somewhere around Deptford, telling us the story of the 1972 Munich Olympics.

'We came third in the team pursuit, but we broke the world record,' he said. 'We crashed in the semi-finals, then we beat the time set by the first-placed team by two seconds. We was gutted.'

Nearing the start line in Greenwich, a gendarme told us to put our lights on, which, given that we were driving in broad daylight, seemed entirely reasonable.

Progress to this point had been swift but comfortable, a cruise through the streets of London that had not offered a single solitary glimpse of a cyclist, but did at least allow us to experience what it must feel like to form part of a royal cavalcade, with thousands of people clapping us for doing precisely nothing.

T-Mobile's Linus Gerdemann ferries water bottles from his team car back to his teammates. Gerdemann went on to win a mountain stage.

Photograph courtesy KM Group

This was about to change. The official start line was opposite the Maritime Museum in Greenwich and, within seconds of the flag dropping, Romain Feillu of the Agritubel team attacked, sending a chain reaction through the cavalcade.

In the *KM* Focus we heard a burst of static and then two words: 'Accelerez! Accelerez!'

Keeble floored the right pedal with extreme prejudice, flinging us back into our seats as the car went from 20 to 50mph in a split second. In hindsight this may not sound that fast, but it was 20mph faster than anyone has ever legally driven on that stretch of road for a very long time. As a passenger it felt like being in the scene from *Star Wars* when the Millennium Falcon first enters hyperspace and the stars suddenly melt into a blur.

Photograph courtesy KM Group

The proximity of the other vehicles added to the sense of clear and present danger.

The term 'minimum stopping distance' was obsolete in the race convoy, which operated as a vehicular peloton, every car and motorbike competing for a few square metres. Gilles overcame the G-force to make an observation. We were doing 50-60mph – there was no possible way the riders could be reaching that kind of speed on the flat.

This was true, Keeble explained, but a racing cyclist can take a corner or negotiate a roundabout without having to decelerate. This corner of south-east London was strewn with road furniture that would slow us down so much that the riders would be impeded unless we used the straight stretches to get a safe distance ahead.

Motorbikes flew in and out of our path, with photographers and race officials hanging off the back as if dangled on elastic.

Not for the first time I thanked a God I had previously shown some reluctance to believe in from sparing me that particular ordeal.

I asked Keeble if his years of riding in a bunch had honed his driving skills. 'No, I just shut my eyes,' he replied. 'I took a policeman's boot off once.'

Our entry into hyperspace might have been delayed but for Feillu's attack, though it was naïve to assume that the peloton would have ambled

Having tackled the first climb of the day the break picks up speed through Southborough.

The peloton on Crescent Road.

TAYLORS
SCAFFOLDING
2 736689

Photograph courtesy Tunbridge Wells Council

Try pedalling that up a hill!

through the opening kilometres when the chance to mount the first breakaway of the 2007 Tour de France was at stake. A counter-attack was launched by Cofidis' Stephane Augé before the A206 reached the Blackwall Tunnel Approach and for the next few miles even the television commentators struggled to keep track of who was off the front. Twelve riders were ahead through Woolwich and Charlton, past the Valley, home of Charlton Athletic. That dozen was whittled down by the time we reached the next sporting landmark, Plumstead High Street, just yards from the former home of the Royal Arsenal Football Club, though only a few bits of terracing in a handful of back gardens and a minute plaque on the site of the old Royal Oak pub now offer any clue that one of the world's biggest football clubs began life there.

The leaders at that point included Augé, the Milram rider Andriy Grivko, Liquigas' Aleksandr Kuchynski, Freddy Bichot of the Agritubel team and, most intriguingly of all, Millar, who used the gentle, tree-lined slope of Bostall Hill to ride away from his companions.

At the back the Australian sprinter Robbie McEwen, one of the hot favourites for the stage, was visibly unconcerned by the prospect of Millar, now in an aerodynamic tuck position with his forearms resting on the tops of his handlebars, building his lead. As he headed down the Woolwich Road into Erith, he built a 15-second advantage.

It had taken no more than a quarter of an hour to get this far. The train would have taken 24 minutes and a car journey, according to the notoriously optimistic AA website, would have been 34 minutes in average traffic. For once the term 'as the crow flies' had some meaning as we were given a glimpse of how short the distance between central London and Kent actually is and how claustrophobic this usually congested nine-mile stretch of road must be.

Whether we were actually in Kent yet was something of a moot point.

Eurosport commentator David Harmon called it as soon as Millar entered Erith, saying, 'We're in Kent proper now. A lot of people consider it south London, but we are in Kent.' But Harmon also mistook the Thames for the Medway estuary, so his geographical knowledge was not absolute. Erith certainly used to be in Kent, as did the start line in Greenwich until 1889, but by 1965 Erith was absorbed into the borough of Bexley and became a part of Greater London.

An emotional attachment to the old county remained via a stubborn insistence on using the term Erith, Kent, in postal addresses, but to someone from outside the M25 the area now feels like part of London, a city which also seems to be set on hoovering up Dartford and Gravesend as it encroaches down the so-called Thames Gateway.

The Mackie-Reynolds and Zak families from London have a picnic during the Tour de France up Goudhurst hill.

People cool off by the pond in Goudhurst.

Millar's lead grew to 30 seconds on his four chasers, who were labouring up a steep hill in central Erith, where the Avenue Road pitch of Erith Town Football Club was decorated by a giant blue bike, visible from hundreds of metres above to the television cameras. But soon the roadside scenery grew bleaker. It was difficult to square the tower blocks on the Northend Road to Crayford with the concept of the Garden of England, but Millar kept ekeing out the seconds, crossing the River Cray with a 44-second advantage as he entered the Borough of Dartford, now unequivocally outside London's political reach and into Kent proper.

Some of the stragglers had to sprint to get back on after misjudging a roundabout and the yellow jersey, Cancellara, could be seen dropping back for mechanical assistance on Victoria Road.

The crowds grew dense again. If they were five deep in the thickest parts of the Bexley section, they were 10 deep in places here.

You could make a case for saying it was the biggest day in the sporting history of almost every town on the race route, and it was certainly possible in Dartford's case. In 1974 the town's football club played in the FA Trophy Final at Wembley, losing 2–1 to Morecambe, but the gate that day was a mere 19,000, of whom a fair percentage were from Lancashire. The town's most famous sporting son of recent times is probably the footballer Glen Johnson. When he broke into the Chelsea first team the editor of one local paper was so overcome with excitement he initiated a weekly 'Glen Watch' feature, which quickly degenerated into an update on how many minutes the right-back had spent sitting on the bench that week and was discontinued long before the most interesting episode of his career, namely when he was arrested in B&Q for shop-lifting (he was later fined £80 for pilfering from the bathroom fittings department, a gratuitous punishment for someone getting by on a few grand a week). The biggest sporting occasion to take place in the town in the recent past was the football club's return to the borough in 2006 after a 14-year exile. A capacity crowd of 4,000 attended the opening game at Princes Park, an event covered by Paul Hobson, who was struck by the devotion of the crowd.

'Easy comparisons with football may be unfair,' he said, 'but my experience at the *KM* had given me an insight into the dedication and emotional commitment of those in the middle-to-lower reaches of the football pyramid, way below the Football League, let alone the Premiership.

'Dartford were then in the Ryman League, Division One South – four divisions below League Two, yet they average more than 1,000 for their home gates in 2007, while crowds [or should that be gatherings?] of three figures are normal for a handful of Kent League clubs.

'Add in Sunday league, school and junior football, multiply this across England's counties and you have an enormous base of those who are intimately involved with, and have a knowledge of, football.

The A28 at Bethersden.

Photograph courtesy KM Group

'While cycling may be the second-fastest growing sport in Britain, only 13,000 people held racing licences as of December 2008, and no more than 25,000 were British Cycling members. While there are clearly more cyclists on the UK's roads than those who are officially affiliated with the sport's governing body, how many were rooting for Cadel Evans, say, or his Predictor-Lotto team come July 2007?'

Hobson backed Matt Rendell's assertion that the Tour was something the uninitiated found a lot easier to get into than other sports.

'I was completely unaware of race tactics,' he admitted. 'Words such as peloton didn't mean anything, despite my French degree, and while jerseys of the yellow variety may be synonymous with the gruelling race, polka dot ones most certainly aren't. Despite some professional swotting up ahead of the time trial and the first stage, le Tour was something of a mystery.

An improvised vantage point on Goudhurst hill.

'This was, I suspect, the position of most of those who came to witness the event in London and Canterbury and everywhere in between, but it was sport as a democratic, unifying force, bringing together whole communities and giving towns as diverse as Woolwich and Tonbridge an equal opportunity to participate in one of the world's most enduring sporting spectacles.'

Hanging out in Goudhurst.

*Team cars navigate
through the hordes.*

There was also, as Hobson observed, a world of difference between watching a bike race on a hot July day and staving off hypothermia while watching Dartford play Waltham Forest in mid-January.

'There seemed to be an acknowledgment that a world-class event had arrived on the doorstep – for many, this was quite literally their doorstep – and it was not to be missed. There was an expectant, exciting atmosphere, no doubt helped by the warm weather. People had brought chairs, picnic rugs and even sofas in preparation for a glimpse of the first stage. There were barbecues and hastily mounted stalls selling drinks. All parts of society had come to catch a glimpse of the riders. They may not have known too much about the intricacies of the Tour, but the British public responded with a carnival.'

Dartford town centre barely registered to Millar, who sped off on the A226 to Swanscombe chewing on a gel, looking almost nonchalant with his forearms again resting on the tops as if the effort of propelling a bike forwards at 30mph was somehow easy.

We were now on the North Kent Rivieira, heading towards Northfleet and the third senior football ground on the route (if you discount the ruins of Arsenal's Manor Ground), Stonebridge Road, home of the team formerly known as Gravesend & Northfleet and now uncomfortably renamed Ebbsfleet United under the terms of a sponsorship deal with Eurostar. Maybe the fans were still reeling from this decision to cash in their identity, but unlike at Charlton a smattering of supporters had turned out in replica shirts to applaud the riders.

Keeble decided this part of the A226 was long and straight enough to take the risk, as he put it, of allowing a few cars to overtake us, and on the long drag into Gravesend we finally saw a tiny pair of pedalling legs.

'We'll be all right as long as I don't p*** these guys off,' he said, referring to a couple of motorcycling gendarmes. 'You can get thrown off the race if they think you're getting in the way.'

There didn't seem much danger of that. We were still at least half a kilometre away from the action. I was just able to make out a lone rider in the colours of the Saunier Duval team and wondered if it might be Millar, but Radio Tour's silence left me in a cocoon of ignorance.

Meanwhile, Eurosport had cut away to broadcast a pre-recorded interview with Mark Cavendish, the 22-year-old sprinter from the Isle of Man who came second in the Canterbury stage of the Tour of Britain and sounded confident to the point of arrogance. It was a welcome quality in a sprinter, though his mood was temporarily shattered when the driver of his T-Mobile team bus decided to play a joke on him by revving the engine and driving off, only to stop a few yards down the road, to the hilarity of his teammates and the commentators, one of whom prophetically said 'Let's hope he doesn't get left behind today.'

The crowds in central Gravesend were breathtaking and up to 15-deep near the clock tower. It seemed that the entire town's population had turned out and again showed how an area can look so different when cars are replaced by people.

Britain's Charly Wegelius, in the green and blue Liquigas kit, can be seen at the left.

Photograph courtesy KM Group

Members of the Bob Roll cult. Roll is a former US professional.

For Matt Davison, this was one of the high points of the day – if not his career. 'Although I knew the race would be coming past my road, actually seeing the television coverage of one of the world's biggest sporting events going past my house was really special,' he said.

His sentiments were obviously shared by his fellow Gravesendians, because a wall of noise hit us as we went through the pedestrian area, an extremely narrow and lightly cobbled section and the closest anyone in the bunch was going to get to feeling they were in Paris-Roubaix.

Despite the fact that he was seemingly yet to break into a sweat, Millar was now 4 minutes and 42 seconds ahead of the main field and nearly two minutes in front of the chasers.

For the first time, on leaving Chalk, we entered open countryside on the road to Higham, not the first place on the race route to cause the French a few pronunciation problems. Unable to pronounce the letter H, confused by the 'i' and thrown completely by the 'gh', Radio Tour's attempt sounded like 'Eeee-urm'.

The village has a population of just under 4,000, according to the 2001 census, a figure that looked something of an underestimate as we drove through, with one eye on the crowds and one eye on the yellow dot we now knew, thanks to one of Radio Tour's sporadic updates, to be David Millar.

Augé takes second place at Goudhurst, with Kuchynski a distant third.

Over at the finish line in Canterbury, the progress of one of the stage favourites was the cause of some concern in the Eurosport commentators' box. 'Robbie McEwen seems to be puffing and blowing a bit,' David Harmon said, before adding, somewhat doubtfully, 'We'll just have to see.'

Back on the road, Millar was approaching the long descent into Strood on the A2 and that meant we needed to *accelerez* all over again, up to 60mph as we screamed down the hill, past a sign that read 'Mad Cows Welcome You To Medway', a subtle piece of political satire that was lost on me at the time due to the proximity of the other race vehicles – which made our speed feel closer to 100mph as we tore along Watling Street into Strood town centre.

Knowing that a sharp left was coming I estimated our chances of actually swinging into North Street without creating a twisted pile of metal, flesh and rubble were around the 50-50 mark.

I did not actually see Keeble use the handbrake, but I can remember being flung against the rear onside window as we came within touching distance of a group of spectators who were getting treated to a rally as well as a bike race.

All the while Millar extended his lead, up to 5m10s on Gun Lane and 5m15s by the time he got to the entrance to the Medway City Estate. Here

CSC lead the field round the corner at the summit of Goudhurst Hill.

he became the first cyclist to, legally at least, ride through the Medway Tunnel, 11 years after its opening, and he continued into Gillingham. The race route studiously avoided the town's major landmark, the Priestfield Stadium, in favour of a faintly uninspiring section via Wharf Road, Pier Road and Medway Road, which included an equally uninspiring, though potentially significant, moment in the race as Millar took the first sprint on Pier Road unchallenged and with it three points for the green jersey competition.

Grivko followed him in second, with Kuchynski third.

It was a smart strategy. The Scot knew he was not going to be able to win in a bunch sprint at Canterbury and was equally aware that the chances of successfully breaking away on Stone Street were minimal due to the sheer speed the bunch would be travelling at by that stage. The small time bonus might also prove significant two or three days down the line. Millar's prologue may have been disappointing, but his proximity to Cancellara left open the possibility that he might snatch the yellow jersey if he got into the right break before the mountains or 'did a ride' in the longer time trial.

The crowds opted for an equally smart strategy on the dual carriageway section. Not knowing which side of the central reservation the race would use, they congregated in the central reservation.

At the front some riders managed to stay in the saddle through Goudhurst, notably Jens Vogt (centre), who bulldozed his way up the fourth category climb.

At a conservative estimate, there were at least 10 people for every metre along the roadside, meaning that in just one kilometre more people were watching a bike race than could cram into Priestfield.

Here Millar's lead peaked at 5m30s, though the television directors found the scenery on the Gillingham/Chatham frontier less than captivating, cutting away to an admittedly spectacular aerial shot of 'Le Chateau d'Upnor' and the Medway Estuary.

One of the joys of Eurosport's coverage was the chance to see Kent from the air. From a vertical vantage point of a few hundred feet Upnor looked breathtaking. From the ground the Medway estuary could be a bewildering mish-mash of warehouses, new housing, rusting boats and mud. This was Dickens territory and on the wrong day the sight of it could be almost as depressing as the thought of starting one of his novels. Even the Chatham ring-road, not the easiest part of the garden of England to love, was a little easier to warm to now that it was clogged with people instead of its usual gridlocked convoy of white van men with one hand on their mobile phones, ignoring their indicators and busily cutting up the stressed-out single parents.

Somebody in the car, almost certainly Keeble, warned us to look out for fishnet stockings and stiletto heels. Millar slowed down to take in the

Crowds begin to mass at the Star & Eagle pub in Goudhurst, site of the second King of the Mountains summit.

Photograph courtesy Colin Flockton

British fans scream encouragement at Millar as he tries to recapture the leaders at Goudhurst.

scenery, to wit some towering orange balloons outside Halfords, or perhaps more realistically to wait for the cavalry to arrive now that he was running out of steam.

On New Road he was just 22 seconds ahead of the chasers, who caught him just after the bridge on New Road Avenue, directly in front of the *Medway News* office, with the peloton now 5m30s back again, ambling past the sprint signs on Pier Road.

Now riding as a quintet, the escapees' lead grew again to 5m35s as they swung around the roundabout into Star Hill, scene of the largest and thickest crowds yet, with row after row of fans stacked upon each other almost as far as the eye could see, looking like the banking at an Indian cricket ground during a one-day international.

Rochester was a lot easier on the eye and as the leaders reached St Margaret's Street, with the peloton, now headed by the CSC team, still meandering along New Road Avenue, the television coverage switched to the aerial shot again, offering a view of 'Le Chateau de Rochester' and 'Le Catedrale de Rochester'.

This was the very spot where I had waited and watched less than 12 months previously, wondering what the hell had happened to the Tour of Britain.

*Fabian Cancellara
(obscured) is either
smiling or grimacing.*

But just as the cameras were really starting to showcase the parts of
Kent where visitors might understand what the fuss was all about, we
cut away to the sight of Vinokourov, changing his bike after a
mechanical mishap on St Margaret's Street. In hindsight it was perhaps
a pity the crowd didn't lynch him, but at the time nobody knew he was
running on something more than energy gel. His Astana team quickly
towed him back to the main field, which at this point was content to let
the breakaway maintain its advantage without allowing it to get to a
potentially alarming level.

From Borstal Road, with its steep concrete banking on one side, the
race convoy passed under the M2 flyover, turned a sharp right onto the
Pilgrims Way and in doing so burst into one of the most open,
panoramic views on the entire route, with the Medway Valley spread-
eagled before us.

Again the aerial shot offered a completely new perspective on such a
familiar area. The North Downs, to the left of the route, offered a series
of apparently impossibly steep byways and bridle paths, strewn with
boulders and tree stumps that could throw you off your mountain bike
or stop you in your tracks if you approached them in the wrong way.
From a helicopter this geographical nightmare for local cyclists looked
like little more than a pimple.

Even the Pilgrims Way itself can slow the average club cyclist down to a crawl. The open, exposed section between Borstal and School Lane has a deceptively difficult gradient and gets battered by unfavourable winds for most of the year. There was something faintly depressing about the way the Tour riders didn't even need to get out of the saddle to cope with this apparent obstacle simply riding at 20mph with their hands on the tops of the bars.

Eurosport cut away again, this time to an interview with five-time Tour winner Bernard Hinault, a Breton with such a countenance that he looked about 48 in his heyday, even though at the time of the 2007 race he was still only 52. Hinault was known for many things during his racing career, but rumours that he had a sense of humour were rarely treated with any more seriousness than the chances of a French yellow jersey contender. His autobiography could have been ghosted by Alan Partridge, a self-justificatory act of defiance that suggested he'd endured rather than enjoyed his career, in the manner of Roy Keane, haunted by any suggestion of failure and unable to actually derive pleasure from his victories for any longer than the moment it took him to cross the finish line.

Bradley Wiggins (left), out of the saddle at Goudhurst. Mark Cavendish is just behind him in the magenta T-Mobile kit with gold glasses.

Photograph courtesy KM Group

If Hinault had ever knowingly cracked a joke there was no public record of it, but he unwittingly made Harmon's co-commentator Sean Kelly, himself no Graham Norton, at least chuckle when he said the point of the race was to 'jouer', or play, and that this stage was 'made for attacks'.

'He was the boss,' Kelly said of Hinault. 'I've seen him when guys go on the attack after a mountain or two mountainous days. He'd go right up to them and say that's not allowed, we're only going to race in the last two hours or 60km, and he did not allow anyone to attack. He was the patron.'

Hinault, Kelly was sure, would not have approved of the way this quintet had attacked virtually from the moment the flag dropped had he been racing, even though he heaped praise on the live wire Claudio Chiappucci. The Italian was yet another rider whose career achievements were effectively rendered meaningless by post-retirement revelations about the fuel he used to power his dare devil attacking style.

Hinault conveniently ignored this, probably because he had retired by the time Chiappucci was proving so difficult for his successors (i.e. LeMond) to keep tabs on.

'I have to laugh when he talks about Chiappucci going on the attack and saying it can be done,' Kelly admitted. 'It certainly makes for good racing, and it makes it easier for us if you have attacks all the time, but it's totally different from the way he envisaged it when he was racing.'

'Nobody warned us about Capel Hill!'

Photograph courtesy KM Group

The next village, Burham, offered evidence that it was not just the francophones who were struggling to pronounce Kentish place names.

Millar and Grivko show the effort after emerging at the top of Capel Hill.

Harmon called it 'Burrr-um', while to the French it was 'BerURM', and to the race organisers it was a handy place to land a few helicopters for a while, half a dozen of them being stationed in a field next to the rec.

The five leading riders extended their lead, past the turn-off for Eccles where several hundred villagers had walked up to watch and along the single carriageway stretch of the Pilgrims Way to Kits Coty, the first part of the route to be entirely devoid of spectators, due to its narrowness (barely wide enough for one vehicle to pass) and the lack of any decent vantage point.

Cyclists with local knowledge will know the section between Kits Coty and the A229 as a short but viciously steep little climb that softens you up before you tackle Blue Bell Hill; either via the cycle path next to the dual carriageway; the old, even steeper route on Warren Road set back from the main road or, if you're feeling suicidal, the dual carriageway itself, which, incredibly, you can still legally ride on.

Four of the breakaway riders were forced out of the saddle for this section, though Millar simply sat down the whole way. As they began the descent into Maidstone the lead was up to 5m47s.

The downhill section of the Pembury by-pass was one of the few spots on the route devoid of spectators.

There were thousands more fans in this area, many watching from the A229 bridge over Rochester Road and some hurdling the central reservation barriers to get a second glimpse of the action, watching the riders disappear under the bridge before emerging on the other side. Even here there was a certain amount of confusion as to the route. Someone followed the French tradition of painting a message on the tarmac, but they miscalculated and chose a section the riders did not actually cover. Over a year later the message remains visible, but it is doubtful anyone has ever been able to read it – it remains etched onto the tarmac on the southbound carriageway, a hundred or so yards before the slip road the riders took to join the A229. Worse still the writing is upside down, so it will only ever be legible to someone peering out of the back seat during one of the periodic traffic jams.

It was here that Keeble decided to give us a glimpse – and it was just a glimpse – of the action, exploiting the widest part of the course so far to pull over by the service station and allow a procession of vehicles and then the five leaders to flash past us, before rejoining the cavalcade behind the team cars. I had no idea who four of these five riders were, though none of them were big hitters. Millar was recognisable enough, but the only other one of the quintet whose name rang even a vague bell was Freddy Bichot, a 28-year-old Frenchman with the Agritubel team, whose sole claim to fame was a stage win and the overall victory in the 2005 Etoile de Bessèges stage race. He was doing his job, which was first to get as much publicity as possible for his team and second to attempt to take out the sprint if, by some miracle, the peloton failed to catch up with them.

Grivko and Kuchynski were simply policemen. The former, a 24-year-old time trial specialist from Sinferopol in the Ukraine, was on sentry duty for Erik Zabel, who was the Milram team's main sprinter in the enforced absence of the Italian Alessandro Petacchi.

This was another classic, cycling-chemistry conundrum. Petacchi had tested 'non-negative' for salbutemol during the 2007 Tour of Italy, and he was consequently declared persona non grata by ASO, though as an asthmatic he at least had a plausible defence, claiming he had merely been trying to relieve his symptoms.

While this was kicking off in Italy, Zabel, now 37, was confessing to using EPO 'briefly' during 1996, in response to allegations made by his former masseur Jef d'Hont in an autobiography. Claiming he had stopped due to side effects, Zabel was not even slapped on the wrist. Eleven years down the line there was obviously no political will left to punish him, so his 200 career wins remain in the record books. The bottom line was that he was free to race, while Petacchi was excluded, later sacked by Milram and handed a one-year ban.

The Tour de France in Sissinghurst. Lynne Boxall and Charlie Harris, serenading race onlookers with bagpipes and a trumpet.

Photograph courtesy KM Group

Had he been allowed to start, however, Petacchi would have been a heavy favourite to win in Canterbury. Zabel was merely a hot tip to finish anywhere in the top 10 other than first. He still had the road sense, the sense of timing and the bike-handling skills needed to get himself into the right positions at the end of a stage, but at 37 his fast-twitch muscles just did not twitch quickly enough anymore. I had lost count of the number of times either Harmon or Liggett had tipped him for a win in the previous two years, only for a handful of younger men to sprint past him in the final metres.

Kuchynski, a Belorussian domestique, or water-carrier, was the Liquigas team's insurance policy in case things did not come together for their playboy sprinter Filippo Pozzato.

Augé was the unknown quantity, an aggressive French rider out to make a name for himself and the main rival to Millar for the day's consolation prizes, the King of the Mountains jersey and the Prix de Combativité for the most attacking rider. There was a sub-plot. He was riding for Cofidis, a French team which, despite being backed by a company of money-lenders, felt it was on firm enough moral ground to sack Millar when he confessed to using EPO in 2004. Millar could hardly have expected anything else, although Augé's presence in the break offered

Liz Grogan gets her face painted with a tiger motif while she waits for the race to hit the village of Sissinghurst.

The bunch turn off the A262 at Sissinghurst.

Photograph courtesy KM Group

him the possibility of putting one over on the team he felt had put him under insufferable pressure to get results.

Of all the thoughts swirling round the riders' heads as they descended into Maidstone, they were at least free from the overriding problem faced by most cyclists trying to traverse the county town, which is trying to get through it with your limbs and equipment intact.

The race entered the town at the Running Horse roundabout and left it at the Barming Bull. Even at off-peak times a cyclist takes his life in his hands if he tries to negotiate the one-way system, the multiple traffic lights, the roundabouts and the four lanes of traffic he needs to cross to clear the town. The cycle lane alternative is fine, provided you want your journey to stop at the Lidl and Matalan superstore.

Only a native can know exactly how it feels to both love and despair of a town at the same time, and there were times when I despaired of Maidstone, my home town and a sporting backwater for as long as anyone could remember.

It was unable to find a home for its football team and unwilling to preserve its crown jewel, the cricket festival, which had been taken away two years beforehand, denying local fans the chance to see a conveyor belt of world stars at The Mote, one of the most attractive grounds in the country.

Photograph courtesy KM Group

*T-Mobile riders off the
back near Tenterden.*

I wondered if Maidstone would 'get' the Tour, given its track record of underachievement, but these fears proved as groundless as Maidstone United, the football team I have supported since childhood and who haven't played a senior game in the county town since 1988. On the descent to the Running Horse spectators were pretty thin on the ground, but by the time the riders emerged from the underpass the roadside was lined again.

An impressive number of Stones fans in amber shirts had congregated by the White Rabbit roundabout, opposite Whatman Way, the site of the ground the club had been six months away from building for the past six years, but this was not the greatest vantage point and this was reflected in the post-race views of those present.

Richard Nott, one local spectator, said 'It was great to see so many Stones fans down there, but wasn't the race over in a second? It was crap.'

Chris Smoker described it as 'the biggest waste of a morning I can remember.'

These, however, were exceptions to the rule.

Bryan Reed of Allington thought it was 'the prefect spectator sport – 30 seconds of intense action and then down to the pub for a well-deserved pint.'

The approach to Tenterden.

*Kuchynski pips Bichot in
the sprint at Tenterden.*

What everyone was agreed on was the brevity of the actual cycling and the conviviality of the atmosphere.

I had brought along a Maidstone United scarf and had planned to wave it to see what, if any, response it got. We had passed Whatman Way before I even managed to get it out of my bag, but by the time we reached Fairmeadow I wafted it out of the window somewhat tentatively, wondering if anyone would notice. The response astonished me. Almost everyone that saw it let out a whoop of delight, making me wonder why our average attendances were only around the 400 mark.

In hindsight I should have realised that this was the Tour de France and people would whoop at a giant cow on the back of a lorry, whose sole reason for existing was to persuade the public to part with cash in exchange for dairy produce.

It was fun while it lasted, however, and it lasted all the way up the Tonbridge Road, past the Cherry Tree where I singularly failed to spot my wife, mother and three-month old daughter and past the Fountain, where I similarly failed to spot my father and 98-year-old grandmother, due entirely to the size of the crowds.

There is a height gain of nearly 100 metres between Lockmeadow and Fountain Lane, but it did not register with the leading five, all of whom spun a high gear as they climbed past the town's most underrated eating establishment, the Charcoal Grill takeaway, and up to 'L'Eglise de St Michel et Tous Les Anges.'

Again Millar simply stayed in the other saddle while the others danced. It looked effortless and the only sign that it had provided any kind of obstacle at all was when the bunch swung into town and clawed back a few seconds from the 5m30s lead.

By the old bridge, one family in particular viewed the sight of this vast, swirling collage of spinning legs as a life-changing experience. Stuart Bradburn was watching the Tour with his family and his father Clive, a member of the San Fairy Ann club. It was the first time they had been out as a family since the death of Stuart's daughter Grace, who was taken to hospital with chicken pox on her first birthday and passed away a month later.

'After Grace's death it would have been understandable if Stuart had shut himself away from the world in a severe state of depression,' Clive said. 'Instead, and I am so proud of him for this, he started to fund-raise and took up cycling. With my vast experience in the sport, a whole two years, I advised him on what type of bike he needed to get out and about and keep himself fit. This he has done and he is now a very accomplished rider.'

The attackers grimace as they leave Bethersden.

*The main field leaves
Tenterden.*

Photograph courtesy Gary King

The peloton roars into Bethersden.

Stuart in fact raised £50,000 for the Intensive Care Unit where his daughter spent her final days in the 12 months after the race and did the London to Paris ride with his father.

Stuart's son, Oliver, was three when he saw the Tour and still talks about 'the day the really fast bikes came past'. On his fourth birthday he discarded the stabilisers on his bike and Clive now allows himself to dream about Oliver becoming a world champion.

Sadly, if Eduardo Gonzalo Ramirez was permitting himself a fleeting dream of the yellow jersey, it was over by the time he reached Royal Engineers Road. At exactly 12.38pm Ramirez, a 23-year-old Spaniard, was trying to get back to the bunch after a mechanical mishap.

The Caisse d'Epargne team car, which had temporarily pulled over, failed to spot him and pulled out into his path. The incident took place right in front of *Kent Messenger* reader Lena Ward, from Ringlestone in Maidstone.

'The cyclist had nowhere to go and went headfirst into the windscreen,' she said. 'It was quite frightening. He landed more or less sitting up and there was glass all over the floor. He was rocking backwards and forwards in pain with blood all over his arm.'

The end is nigh: a motorcyclist holds up a blackboard, telling the break its lead is coming down rapidly.

Paramedics were on the scene within a minute, but the game was up for Ramirez. Cyclists regard finishing a race as a point of honour and will ride through mortal agony to avoid quitting. In William Fotheringham's book *Roule Brittania* Tom Simpson's mechanic Harry Hall recalled the former World Champion's bike being 'covered in sh*t' during an early stage of his fateful 1967 Tour de France as he tried to shrug off diarrhoea.

Paul Kimmage wrote of an overpowering stench when riding near a similarly stricken Greg LeMond in 1986, and a year later Sean Kelly broke down in tears when he was forced to abandon the race with a broken collarbone. Cristiano Ronaldo might collapse like a Jenga tower whenever the wind gets above 5mph, but a Tour rider will attempt to defy the inevitable like John Cleese in *Monty Python and the Holy Grail*.

Ramirez was luckier than Cleese in the sense that he did not lose four limbs, and he was probably yelling 'mierda' rather than 'Tis but a scratch.

Have at ye!', but five minutes after the crash he was only able to pedal for a few yards after remounting. Clutching his ribs he ground to a halt again and abandoned the race, the first casualty of the 2007 Tour, less than halfway through its first stage.

CSC remained on the front of the bunch, but as they ascended the Tonbridge Road, the escapees began to build their lead again on the descent into Barming and the fast stretch of the A26 out towards the second sprint of the day in Teston – or 'Test On', as both ITV and Eurosport's commentators described it.

This was one of the more understandable errors, as the county's place names are governed by unknowable rules, presumably made up by illiterate locals a few hundred years ago in a bid to catch out strangers. Just as the casual visitor is asked to believe Trotiscliffe is pronounced 'Trosley', so certain locals insist Teston should be 'Teeson', but it wasn't David Harmon's fault that an 18th-century signwriter didn't know how to spell, nor that no one had bothered to correct him since.

The road into the village flattens out as it runs parallel to the Medway Valley, with Teston Bridge to the south and Barham Court to the north. Just before the village proper, after the junction with the B2163, the road

The tail-end Charlies need to get out of the saddle.

Photograph courtesy Gary King

kicks up brutally for the casual cyclist, but almost unnoticeably to David Millar, although he did do local cyclists the honour of finally getting out of the saddle for this momentum-killing stretch up to the Crown City Chinese restaurant.

What happened next illustrates just how drastic the difference in perspective can be between the fanatical and the disinterested.

To the casual television viewer, Millar simply glanced over his shoulder, began sprinting 100 metres from the sign that marks the border between Teston and Wateringbury and easily stayed clear of a half-hearted challenge from Grivko. To Martyn Peal it was a moment of epiphany.

'I knew there was going to be a sprint at Wateringbury, but I'd conditioned myself not to expect anything because nine times out of 10 they're a non-event. There's a breakaway and all the riders are trying to get time, so nobody goes for the points, but one in 10 times something happens.'

Bethersden lies in wait. Decorative bikes hang from the walls of a house opposite the Bull in Bethersden.

Photograph courtesy Gary King

His faith was rewarded. Rumours that David Millar was on the attack had reached Peal's vantage point, by the sign on the A26 that marks the end of Teston and the beginning of Wateringbury.

A flash of Millar's yellow uniform in the distance confirmed these were true. 'I saw this figure clad in yellow and thought, that's David Millar. Then I thought, he's going to go for it! And he went for it and I had tears streaming down my cheeks, as did a mate of mine, Derek Howlett.'

If Peal was overwhelmed, not all of his neighbours felt the same. 'For someone who knows the sport it was fantastic, because when the main field came through I could see the CSC team, the Discovery team etc all flying past, but a family I know didn't really understand what the fuss was about.'

So he put it in terms they could understand: 'They were into football so I said "You're Liverpool fans right? Well it's like having Liverpool play at Wateringbury rec."'

The penny dropped, though Peal wasn't hanging around to convert any more non-believers. He got in his car and bombed down to Capel, where once again his emotions got the better of him.

He was not the only spectator to use local knowledge to his advantage. Graham Galpin of Ashford, having ridden the cyclo-sportive stage a week before, had a place in the VIP enclosure at Rochester Castle. Once the race had passed, he foreswore the complimentary drinks, sprinted over the Medway Bridge to Strood, where he had left his car to avoid the road closures, drove to his brother-in-law's house in Ashford, changed into his cycling gear and rode into the town centre to meet his family. From there he watched the race on television, jumped outside as it came past and then rode 'head down' to Canterbury, just in time to see the finish.

Photograph courtesy KCC

Kent's art students celebrated the Tour's arrival in a number of ways.

Chapter 14

KELLY ZEROES

To a seasoned race observer like Sean Kelly, the writing was already on the wall for the break. 'It's very early for the gap to be coming down and it's very unlikely they'll stay away,' he observed, as the quintet were clocked at 5m10s in front at the junction of Pizien Well Road and the A26.

That tumbled by another five seconds as the bunch reached Teston and was down to 5m00s when they got to the Wateringbury crossroads.

Another aerial shot gave viewers a glimpse of the opulent private gardens between Wateringbury and Mereworth, virtually invisible from the roadside, and a shot of Mereworth church inspired the commentators to break off from a discussion about the merits of porridge and rice pudding as race fuel to laud the countryside. At Mereworth, an already sizable crowd was swelled by the members of the West Peckham cricket club, whose fixture had been cancelled when their opponents said they couldn't reach the ground.

This was, one team member told me, almost certainly bullsh*t, as the Medway-based side only needed to make a minor diversion to get to West Peckham village green. Instead, with varying degrees of enthusiasm, the West Peckham team turned up in the neighbouring village, home of their fiercest rivals, to watch the German Stefan Schumacher dangle off the back.

Once again, with the benefit of hindsight, it really is a pity Schumacher's fondness for substances stronger than rice

Photograph courtesy KM Group

pudding wasn't more widely known at the time, as he might have got the lynching his positive test for CERA, a designer form of EPO, during the 2008 Tour suggests he deserved.

Kuchynski, Bichot and Augé attempt to stay clear through Ashford.

With Jens Vogt, an altogether more likable German rider, organising the chase for the CSC team, the lead might have tumbled below the 5m00s mark, but as they approached Goose Green on the run into Hadlow there was a break for what the French politely call 'raisons naturelles'.

By the time they had climbed back on and reached 'Le Chateau d'Hadlow' the break were 5m28s ahead again and in the outskirts of Tonbridge.

'Isn't this where the angry people come from?' Harmon asked, clearly confused. 'Angry of Tunbridge Wells?'

He'd be angry too if he had to cycle on roads like these. There are individual ruts on the Hadlow Road worthy of a fourth category mountain classification.

I had stashed my Maidstone scarf away at this point as this was the territory of our main rivals, the Tonbridge Angels, and wafting something black and amber from the window would have been tantamount to spray-painting a target on the side of the car.

Tonbridge does, however, boast the best rail service to Kent from London and despite the fact that South Eastern Trains had, brilliantly, decided to ban passengers from taking bikes with them on the day itself, the town was packed with natives and day-trippers. It was also the one part of the route to have experienced something similar in recent memory. Less than three years previously the roads were gridlocked with pedestrians for a civic reception for Kelly Holmes, who had just returned from Athens with two Olympic gold medals, arguably the greatest sporting feat by anyone from the county, though David Sadler of Yalding and Manchester United and Baron Cowdrey of Tonbridge could also stake serious claims to that title.

As the leaders made their way through the High Street at at least four times the average speed any car would be able to negotiate it in even off-peak traffic, the conversation in the commentary box turned to one of the contenders for overall victory.

'Boonen is targeting the stage win and has ambitions to snatch the jersey,' said Eurosport's Emma Davies, before revealing: 'But he's apparently allergic to pollen and was affected by it in Hyde Park.'

This statement earned a post-dated irony a few months later when Boonen was troubled by another substance that can affect the sinuses, namely the cocaine he was busted for in an out-of-competition test 11 months later, an episode that also lent a fresh perspective to Boonen's occupation of the moral high ground during the 2006 Tour of Britain.

'I love Sarcozy's nose...'
(sic)

The bunch pass Ashford International. The Saunier Duval riders are trying to reel in Stéphane Augé and preserve Millar's lead in the King of the Mountains competition.

At the time, however, there was every reason to believe Boonen would win the stage, with the CSC team keeping the break at a safe distance, heading into Tonbridge on the Hadlow Road, just as the quintet started tackling the first official climb of the day.

I was sceptical about Quarry Hill's claims to fourth-category status and was glad when Keeble was equally scathing, saying he time-trialled up its 130 metres above sea level for fun in his spare time.

The crowd was six deep at the foot of the hill, where Millar was again riding almost contemptuously in the saddle, though he did stretch his legs a little as he crossed the bridge over the A21.

The road, unsatisfyingly for a supposed climb, flattened out significantly, allowing the five to shift into their larger chain rings again. Millar, spinning his legs furiously, dived away from the other four to reach the summit first and take the lead in the King of the Mountains competition ahead of Grivko and Kuchynski, though only after a far harder effort than he had needed to make at Teston.

Davies, meanwhile, was discussing the chances of another Briton. 'Cav seemed very nervous,' she said. 'And he's obviously feeling the pressure. He was second in the Tour of Britain stage here last year because he took the wrong line and went the wrong way around the roundabout, so he's hoping others will make the mistake he did.

Bradley Wiggins (in the red and white top with red sunglasses) had a relatively easy day in the bunch, after the disappointment of coming third in the London Prologue.

'Brad's [Wiggins] phone was off last night. He was very, very disappointed and everyone left him alone. He said this morning that he'd got over it and was determined to do something today, but I think Cav's going to win.'

The 'Côte de Southborough' had slowed the five down to the point that their lead was only 4m45s at the top, where television viewers were briefly treated to shots of Southborough cricket ground, 'L'Eglise King Charles the Martyr' and Dunlorlan Park, but is was back to 4m53s at St Johns, where the feeding station spread out for almost a kilometre along the A26.

For the only time during the day, dark clouds were gathering overhead and Keeble decided it was time for another wind-up. 'If it rains, they'll all pull over and get mudguards from their team cars,' he said, duping the credulous Gilles, who was about to go live on air with this scoop until the tittering from elsewhere in the car gave the game away.

The helicopter view of central Tunbridge Wells showed crowds at their deepest yet, with drinkers spilling out of the Pitcher and Piano pub and trying to sprint up to Mount Pleasant Road in time to see the race pass by. Not all of them made it, judging by the footage of tiny dots moving unpredictably, as if down on the ground they were already too lashed up to remember where the riders were supposed to be.

And then there were three: Augé, Bichot and Kuchynski mount an act of defiance outside Ashford.

Kuchynski leads through the country lanes south of Ashford.

At this point Matt Davison allowed himself a few minutes out of the studio to sample the ambience.

'You can only stand in one spot, but you see the carnival, you see all the mobiles going past and then you see the cyclists,' he said. 'They go by in a wink, but you don't feel cheated, even though it's taken them less than a minute to go by. You get such a happy atmosphere there, which is not like other sports. The size of the crowd was like you'd get at a Premier League football match, but at football a section of the crowd are going to be disappointed because their team has lost. It was a strange feeling because so many people were there, but nobody really cared who won, they just wanted to be a part of it.'

On the way out of town on the Pembury Road the crowds thinned to the point that by the time the race reached the A228 the roadside was completely deserted on the long downhill to the Old Church Road turn-off, though they were back in force for the steep uphill section to Hawkwell Farm.

Steeper still was the imminent arrival of Capel Hill, or Crittenden Road, to give it its official, less revealing name. I wondered aloud why the organisers had not graded this one as fourth category and Keeble did not waste any time agreeing. 'Capel is a b******,' he stated, knowing full well that there might only be a height gain of around 60 metres, but that it was enough to do serious damage to the unsuspecting rider.

Lulling the peloton into a false sense of security, two women had wheeled a pair of armchairs down their driveway (not a meagre feat in this part of the county) to watch the race while enjoying a picnic.

While the peloton was freewheeling down the Pembury by-pass, all hands on the brake hoods, even Millar was forced to stand on the pedals as he coped with both the gradient and Martyn Peal's attempts to keep pace with him on foot.

The speed, 10mph at one point, was the slowest the riders would drop to all day and the hill should have put a dent in the lead, but by the top the five were 5m33s ahead and with the bunch taking another natural break by Redwings Lane it grew to 6m03s as they hammered through Matfield to Brenchley, where they were met by a deafening chorus of claxons and six-deep crowds, who congregated at bends and junctions.

In the latter village someone, hopefully with knowing irony, had painted 'Come on Henman!' on the road.

Sean Kelly at least had recognised this was nobody's idea of a flat stage. 'It's quite undulating,' he admitted. 'If you rode this for 100k you'd know you'd ridden a bike. It's certainly not flat. When you're in a bunch you go downhill at very fast speeds and go very fast at the tops of the hills. For training purposes this would be a very heavy ride, so some riders may suffer.'

Grivko leads, moments before he and Millar decided to sit up.

Photograph courtesy KM Group

Augé tries to keep the break going on the A28 between Tenterden and Ashford.

Photograph courtesy KM Group

Crowds gather on Canterbury's city wall.

Harmon agreed and talked up the difficulty posed by Farthing Common, though the unanimous feeling was that it was too far from the finish to really affect the result.

They were equally unanimous about the scenery, with everyone purring about the views of the Weald and the turn-out, though, as Millar et al passed through Horsmonden, Harmon confessed to being staggered at the news that one of the world's top five sparkling wines was allegedly produced in Kent.

The whine of burning brake pads was audible as the breakaway bombed down Spelmonden Road, a high-speed descent with the kind of left-hander an inexperienced rider would struggle to tackle alone, let alone in the middle of 200 rivals.

As we swung onto the A262, it was obvious that my Goudhurst Tour experience was going to be vastly different to the 1994 let down.

'Bloody hell, Vietnam!' Keeble blurted, as he caught sight of the helicopters swarming above the village, known as 'Goooderrst' to the French.

This was as close as we were going to get to the feeling of watching a mountain stage in France.

The roadside was choked with pedestrians of multiple nationalities: Danes with red-and-white faces, some of them painted, some just sun-

Photograph courtesy KM Group

Patriotic deck chairs at the finish line in Canterbury.

burned, orange-clad Dutchmen, Belgians waving the Flandrian flag, a black lion on a yellow background, and a smattering of Americans and Anzacs amid the Europeans.

Millar may have been distracted by the spectacle, or he may just have been exhausted, but he made a tactical error at the foot of the hill, where he was caught out by a surprise attack from Bichot. All four rivals gave chase, but Millar was off the back at the 30mph signs at the entrance to the village, while Augé was burying himself to get back on. He did, only for Bichot to calmly pedal away from him to take maximum points for the King of the Mountains prize.

The line, oddly, was not at the very top of the hill (126 metres above sea level), but was instead by the Star & Eagle pub, which had been turned into an impromptu terrace, along the lines of Henman Hill at Wimbledon.

With Kuchynski taking third and with it the final point, Millar had left himself vulnerable to an attack on the final climb of the day. Although he was still leading the polka-dot jersey classification on a tie-breaker, his overall position being higher than Kuchynski's, his companions could snatch the jersey from him if they still led at that point.

If they had been reeled in by an attack from one of the 12 riders ahead of him in the general classification that might also deny him his moment on the podium, though he did at least look in better shape than Grivko, who had seemingly been cut adrift and left for dead.

'It was a little tougher than the route book gives it credit for,' Harmon reflected as the quartet gathered their breath, their lead trimmed by 30 seconds. 'Although Bichot was hard at it, all the other riders were grinding to a halt.'

ITV's Gary Imlach and Ned Boulting watch in horror as Cavendish's Farthing Common mishap is shown.

Photograph courtesy KM Group

A junior peloton formed
part of the pre-race
entertainment in
Canterbury.

It was at this point that trouble of a different kind befell a local farmer. Sixty-year-old Brian Henley was arrested and cuffed for allegedly interfering with road signs and swearing in front of children. He admitted the first charge, while denying the second.

'I did not swear, but I do admit that I did throw the road signs and that is why I was arrested. But they were in the wrong place,' he told Emily Hall of the *KM*. 'I told the officer to speak to his superiors and move himself but he was totally inflexible and quite arrogant. My axe to grind was that the road had been closed three miles from where it should have been and lots of people had to walk unnecessarily because of it.'

Henley had a point. Bedgebury Road should have been closed at the junction with Peasley Lane, just a short walk from the village centre, but instead visitors faced an hour's hike and some apparently missed the race. It was a cock-up, but given the sheer numbers of people swamping the county it says something about the way Kent Police handled the day

KCC put out thousands of yellow signs warning of road closures – all of which were taken as souvenirs by spectators.

that this was the worst recorded incident. Over a thousand other junctions were successfully shut and Henley was quickly 'de-arrested', whatever that means.

Other farmers had more joy, hiring out their fields for people to use as car parks, and back on the course rumours of Grivko's demise proved exaggerated. He recovered before his rivals reached Wilsley Pound, though their hopes now looked increasingly slim.

Team CSC had clearly decided the leaders had been dangling out in front for long enough and Goudhurst Hill was not going to prevent them reeling them in. Jens Vogt led the bunch, like Millar sitting in the saddle throughout, though that was the only similarity with the Scot's style. Vogt simply powered his way up the slope in an efficient, German way, dragging everyone along in his wake and shelling a few people out at the back.

TOUR de FRANCE SUN 8 JULY

POLICE

❌ No stopping Midnight - 7 pm SUN 8 JULY

Parked vehicles liable to removal

Photograph courtesy KM Group

'It's quite a big hill,' an impressed Kelly remarked, before giving his tips for the stage win. 'Cav, [Bernhard] Eisel, McEwen can do it even without a team, [Oscar] Friere, Benati, Robert [Forster], [Thor] Hushovt…'

With Vogt still tugging the field along, the lead was cut to 4m28s as the bunch hit Wilsley Pound and 4m19s when they reached Sissinghurst, where another San Fairy Ann member, Pat Hill, chose to watch.

Hill, an émigré from the East End of London, had been cycling around the Weald for the previous four decades. She too had worried that her enthusiasm for the race might not be shared, but her fears evaporated when she and her husband parked up at 10am in a nearby field for £3 – others used a park and ride option from 'le Chateau de Sissinghurst', which was also shown from the helicopters.

Sissinghurst was not about to spurn its moment in the global spotlight. Stilt walkers, dancers, steam engines and marquees all barred their route.

'I soon saw that my inane question to a local lady a few days earlier as to whether there would be parking and something to eat on the race day was a bit unnecessary,' Hill recalled. 'As I strolled through the village in the sunny hours we had to spare before the race, having bagged our places on the barriers manned by police who, both here and with the many thousands of fans in London, had no drunken hooligans to worry about, I looked at familiar old Sissinghurst with new eyes.'

Canterbury's old city wall.

This was a fairly common experience among race-goers. It was an epiphany to be outdoors without the omnipresent automobile. All right, they weren't bad at getting you around, but what was the price? At Sissinghurst, Hill was able to see the village without the noise, smell, pollution or the fear of getting mown down.

'I really "saw" the lovely cottages, the colourful gardens, and all the front doors open with tables and chairs out ready for the day's enjoyment and I would like to express my personal thanks to all the villagers who put on such a grand show for the hundreds of visitors,' she said.

And in a counter-blast at those who had launched pre-emptive complaints about being prisoners in their own homes, Hill wrote to the *Kent Messenger*, saying 'I wish those who have moaned in your pages about being confined to their houses for hours could have seen the people, many old and obviously not cyclists, lining the route.

Photograph courtesy KM Group

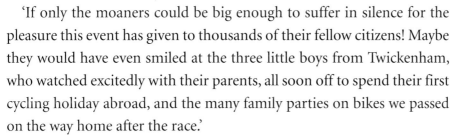

The Hawkinge posse arrives.

'If only the moaners could be big enough to suffer in silence for the pleasure this event has given to thousands of their fellow citizens! Maybe they would have even smiled at the three little boys from Twickenham, who watched excitedly with their parents, all soon off to spend their first cycling holiday abroad, and the many family parties on bikes we passed on the way home after the race.'

Touché, although my own experience of Sissinghurst wasn't quite as positive.

After exiting the centre we were on Chapel Lane, heading for Golford, when Keeble informed us 'Next lay-by, I'm stopping.'

He did his own version of the swerve Michael Schumacher performed on Damon Hill to stop him winning the 1994 Formula 1 World Title, veering violently into a lay-by pockmarked with craters. The Focus's front onside wheel hit one with a suspension-shattering smack and the four of us were flung forwards, kept in one piece only by

The Tour de France arrives in Canterbury. The scene at Wincheap roundabout.

our seatbelts. 'I'm just breaking it in – it's only got 18 miles on the clock,' was Keeble's defence.

Up until that point I had not needed a natural break, though that was rectified by this kamikaze manoeuvre.

Through Golford the lead tumbled drastically to 3m29s. Millar was trying to organise his companions and his untroubled style moved Kelly to suggest that he might have enough left in the tank to make one final move.

He certainly looked a better bet than Augé, who was 'bobbing' violently, wasting energy by fighting his bike as much as he was trying to propel it forwards.

Through the Hemsted Forest the gap came down at a rate of several seconds per kilometre. It dipped below three minutes for the first time in a deserted section around Fosten Green and was 2m46s as they crossed the Kent & East Sussex Railway Line, which offered one of the most iconic images of the day, as a steam train saluted the Tour with that rich, deep whistle that once announced the service from Headcorn to Tenterden and down to Rolvenden and Robertsbridge. The railway had not seen active service since 1961, its closure pre-dating even Dr Beeching's lobotomy of the British railway network. The whistle, which could be heard in the town centre, was deliberate – tipping off the thousands in the centre that the riders' arrival was imminent.

Had they followed the original planned route, the noise might have been even louder, as the line planned to send two locomotives to the level crossing on the A28. Instead, an alteration sent the race up Cranbrook Road, where only one loco was on hand to give a salute, though the 'terrier' tank that saluted the riders was seen on both ITV and Eurosport and as a result the K&ESR received emails from enthusiasts all over the world. It also saw a surge of business. One of Kent Police's brighter sparks had approached the K&ESR, now run as a tourist line, via Kent County Council, with the idea of running a park and ride scheme on the day of the race. The line's general manager Graham Baldwin, who was also heavily involved in organising the celebrations in the town itself, readily agreed, though on the morning of the race he was starting to wonder if it had been such a good idea.

'Our chairman rang me at 9am from Rolvenden to say he'd been there for half an hour and there wasn't a single person there,' he recalled. 'I said that there'd been a lot of interest and that he shouldn't worry.'

Some of the densest crowds were to be found in Tunbridge Wells.

Photograph courtesy Tunbridge Wells Council

In fact just four people had pre-booked for the service from Bodiam, but Baldwin's faith was vindicated before the telephone conversation was even over.

'He said he could see the first five cars coming in, and from then on we were very busy.'

Unprecedentedly busy. A diesel service with a full complement of 70 passengers arrived at Tenterden Town and a ripple of excitement went through the staff, all of whom were enthusiasts who worked on the line for nothing more than the love of it. Baldwin ceased worrying about losing money and began to fret about the line's capacity to cope instead. 'Only one family had bought a pre-booked ticket from Bodiam, but I got a phone call saying the 11.25 train was nearly full when it left there,' he said. 'So I rang Northiam and "thought this is going to be interesting". They told me there were another 100 people waiting to get on there. At Rolvenden it was like a tube train at Oxford Circus in the rush hour.'

'In health and safety terms it was marginal,' he added, with some measure of understatement.

Baldwin sent as many trains back as he could to pick up stragglers until the police intervened and 'invited' him to shut the line. 'We could have brought another 50 or 60 passengers,' Baldwin estimated, and he doesn't know if these people got to see the race.

Winding up for the sprint in Canterbury.

Having surged ahead of his rivals, McEwen veers to the right of the road.

He himself walked up the hill to watch the race from an upstairs window on the High Street, then walked back to find himself in the middle of what he described as 'a football crowd'.

For the first time in the preservation-era, they had to shut the gates at Tenterden Town. Baldwin also believes it is unlikely this ever happened when the railway was part of the national network: 'It was really just for sheep and men on bikes back then. The only comparable events are our Thomas the Tank Engine Days – and they're pre-booked.'

In all, 887 passengers used the railway on 8 July and the race indirectly left a permanent legacy for Tenterden's social calender.

The more clued-up traders in the Chamber of Commerce realised this was a serious commercial opportunity and organised an event on Tenterden rec with live music, trick cyclists and other events.

An estimated 10,000 people watched the race in the town itself and the support events proved so successful that by 2008 it was restaged, minus the Tour, as the 'Tentertainment' festival, which seems certain to become an annual event.

Photograph courtesy KM Group

McEwen, head down, surges past Boonen.

Baldwin, looking back on the day, describes it as a 'fantastic' occasion for the line and one that delighted the K&ESR staff, who were thrilled to see the line heaving with customers.

Heaving of a different kind was on the minds of the race leaders.

The five riders were slowed, as a thousand club runs had been, by a deceptive rise into Tenterden itself, where Millar did not bother to contest the sprint in the High Street, allowing Kuchynski to claim first place, ahead of Bichot and Grivko.

That briefly boosted the lead to 2m49s, but with the sprinters' teams now scenting blood, a fully organised chase was in full cry.

At 'L'Eglise de St Michel et Tous les Saints' Lotto and Credit Agricole had moved to the front, shaving almost half a minute off the leaders' advantage in less than a mile. Unity in the front group disintegrated when Bichot attacked, to the supreme uninterest of his four rivals.

Chapter 15

THE END IS NIGH

By the time the Eurosport crew had given their final, final predictions – Harmon and Mike Smith plumping for Cavendish, Kelly going for McEwen – Bichot had been reeled in again and the organisers had given their equivalent of a Roman Emperor pointing a downward thumb at a gladiator, by telling us to get out of the no man's land between the leaders and the bunch.

It was breakfast revisited time again as Keeble floored the pedal and flung us back into our seats.

We got a glimpse of Millar, locked in conversation with his directeur sportif in High Halden, our second and final sight of the action from the car, before tearing along the A28 towards Ashford.

The breakaway was suffering something of a lingering death. The bunch was poised to cut the gap to within two minutes when it was slowed by a crash in High Halden, where Brett Lancaster, Xavier Zandio, Christian Moreni and Juan Mercado could all be seen picking bits of a traffic island out of their legs.

By Bethersden the lead was temporarily back up to 2m27s, but Millar had had enough. He entered the village with his four long-time companions, but was off the back by the time he left the parish, as he and Grivko decided to sit up.

Crowds on the A28 outside the village were sparse, barring a woman from Glasgow who had reportedly driven all the way down from Scotland with 'three children, two dogs and one husband.' She was able to witness the Lotto team of Robbie McEwen, whose tenuous local connections extended to a Scottish name and a British passport, even though he was as Australian as a bad soap opera, taking charge of the chase.

Millar and Grivko were swallowed up by the bunch as they passed the church at Great Chart, but the defiant trio were clinging to a 1m56s lead that they extended by five seconds as they entered the outskirts of Ashford. At the Prince Albert pub it was back under two minutes again and at the international station just 90 seconds separated them from the chasers.

*The Stage 1 finish line,
Canterbury.*

Realising the danger to Millar's King of the Mountains lead, Saunier Duval began to assist the chase through the town centre.

There was a different atmosphere in the railway town, as unlike in Rochester, Maidstone and Tunbridge Wells, there didn't seem to be any obvious focal point. This was partly down to the route and perhaps partly down to the way Ashford has evolved, with its town centre's influence steadily eroded by the sheer number of retail parks at its perimeter. Two decades ago Ashford was tipped to become a major south-eastern city, thanks to the Channel Tunnel. News organisations credulously reported predictions that the population would rise to 250,000, though by 2001 the official figure was only just into six figures.

False expectations also haunted Ashford Town FC. In the year 2000 the former Manchester City star Rodney Marsh was briefly involved with a group looking to take over the club. He made a solitary visit to their Homelands stadium, predicted the Nuts & Bolts would quickly win promotion to the Football League, and was never seen again. In fact, Marsh's prediction was one of the less ludicrous aspects of his involvement at Homelands. In theory there was no reason why a town of Ashford's size shouldn't support a team at Conference level, but with average gates struggling to top the 200 mark and a stadium four miles outside the town the reality was Ryman Division One South football for the foreseeable future.

The town did have individual success stories, however. Aside from Jamie Staff it could boast of the cricketer Mark Ealham, the future Olympic 1,500-metre finalist Lisa Dobriskey and erm, Neil Ruddock, whose inclusion in this list hinges on widening one's interpretation of the word 'success' to include the kind of footballer who could pass himself off as a poor man's Vinnie Jones.

The race skirted the old shopping centre, instead following the apparently endless dual carriageways down Romney Marsh Road, where people were still two deep, but seemingly subdued by the barriers, with the exception of a few game mountain-bikers who were attempting – and failing – to keep up with the leaders on the other side of the central reservation.

Robbie McEwen spreads his arms like a Messiah as he completes his astonishing comeback to take the win. Tom Boonen looks non-plussed in third.

Robbie McEwen of Australia wins the stage in Canterbury.

Even now, with the end nigh, the trio were still moving at around 30mph, making them easy meat for the chasing pack, though the flailing efforts of the mountain bikers illustrated to the uninitiated just how hard it is to propel a bike at such a speed on the flat.

At the turn off to Church Hill the lead dipped under a minute for the first time and it was 51 seconds as the bunch crossed the A2070.

At Bliby, Bichot exhorted his companions to make a final effort and they briefly pushed the gap back over the minute mark to the bunch and further to the American Levi Leipheimer, who had dropped off the back on Finn Farm Road for an ill-timed pit stop. But it did not last. The advantage began to fall so quickly that in the time it took the race organisers to write '50 seconds' on a blackboard and send a motorbike out to hold it up in front of the leaders, the television cameras were reporting it was down to 35, then 20 as the riders swung right on to the A20.

Britain's Liquigas rider Charly Wegelius made a rare appearance at the front, though it was difficult to tell if he was smiling or grimacing.

The question was now 'where' rather than 'when'. For Kuchynski and Grivko the answer was opposite Apple Barn in Smeeth, one of the few places on the route the French could actually pronounce and the home of the *Kent on Sunday* media group.

Augé had ditched them on the A20 and was pulling away again, even though it looked like he was fighting a tractor beam. He had 32 seconds at Sellindge as he turned into Swan Lane, and a trio of Saunier Duval riders were attempting to haul him back.

Chapter 16

CHUTE! CHUTE!

The section between Sellindge and the top of Farthing Common defined the stage. On this four-mile stretch of road, from the A20 to the top of the North Downs, two of the favourites for the stage win crashed and the responses of their respective teams delivered an object lesson in the art of teamwork – as did Saunier Duval's nursing of David Millar.

Radio Tour broke the news: 'Chute! Robbie McEwen!' and the cameras showed him, Fabien Wegman, Kurt Asle Arvesen and Thomas Voeckler in disarray on Blindhouse Lane, along with Dario Cioni, the Italian rider who was born in Berkshire. With 22.6km to go, crashing at the foot of the day's biggest climb was potentially terminal for the Australian's chances of taking the sprint, but there was no discernible sign of panic as

The rest of the bunch trail in.

he remounted, gripped the hoods of his handlebars and began the chase.

Teammate after teammate received the news on their radios and one by one they dropped back to assist. Assuming the drama was over, the cameras switched back to the front of the race, where Augé was beginning the steep section of the climb from the Pilgrims' Way with a 27-second lead over the bunch, making a phenomenal effort to stay out ahead, flitting in and out of the saddle and swinging his handlebars from side to side, his face betraying the physical ordeal he was suffering.

And then disaster. 'Chute! Mark Cavendish!'

Cut to third and final motorbike camera and the Manxman screaming in mental rather than physical anguish, his T-Mobile helmet pushed halfway up his head, his face the same magenta colour as his team's garish jerseys.

Photograph courtesy CCC

A wincing Robbie McEwen climbs onto the podium, cuts visible on his knee.

'Oh no, that's Mark Cavendish!' yelled a distraught David Harmon. 'Oh no, what's happened? He's lost a chain, that's absolutely desperate.'

Out on the route, San Fairy Ann rider Keir Williams, from nearby Stanford, suspected something was up.

'I knew that the climb would be really busy, and with my wife, baby son and parents, we decided to walk from home to a narrow country lane which comes out just before the bottom of the hill,' he recalled. It was one of the thinnest sections on the stage and Williams knew a bottleneck was likely. 'I remember the helicopters hovering for ages before the race finally reached us, and the peloton moving at a fair pace, but due to the narrowness of the road, the jostling for positions before the climb had already mostly taken place,' he said. 'A couple of minutes after the riders passed, the team car came hurtling along, passing the other team cars, and later I discovered that Mark Cavendish had been knocked off about half a mile up the road, just at the bottom of the climb, hence the car's frantic pace to reach him.'

Robbie McEwen – race winner.

Cavendish had lost more than a chain. His teammates had vanished down the road and his temper – and any chance of getting back on – had disappeared with them.

Not for the first time, T-Mobile's surfeit of team leaders clouded their judgement at a critical moment. In 2005 they blew a distant shot at the general classification when Vinokourov, Kloden and Ullrich rode against each other in the mountains, instead of ganging up on Armstrong. Now they abandoned Cavendish to his fate, assuming he was too far gone to stand a realistic chance in the sprint and instead pinned their hopes on Eisel.

Lotto's strategy was more simple. With one shot at the stage win and one shot only, there was no option but to drop back and help McEwen regain the bunch, and if it didn't work, there would always be the next stage.

For T-Mobile, a British stage-winner in a British stage of the Tour de France would potentially have been worth millions in terms of publicity and profile, but Cavendish suffered fresh mechanical complications when he remounted and was reduced to thumping his handlebars in frustration.

Back in the commentary positions in Canterbury, the Eurosport team sounded almost as distraught as Cavendish. 'He's almost in tears, I can't believe it,' Harmon wailed. 'He's got to stay calm – he can't go charging up there like a madman because he won't have anything left for the sprint.'

But there would be no sprint – and there was no 'almost' about Cavendish's tears.

He later told *The Guardian*'s Donald McRae, 'It was 25km from the finish and I was up at the front. If I had been further back I would've been OK. The next thing I know I'm lying on the ground. I hit a woman. Apparently she had been told to stand back throughout the day. It's great that she wanted to watch but people are not aware how the sport works over here.'

Cavendish's head clearly was not right. In an earlier report he claimed he had hit a man, though the gender of his assailant was largely irrelevant given he had just seen the chance of a lifetime killed off by a single act of stupidity. And he did not bother putting a brave face on it for McRae. 'You can see on TV that I'm gutted, I'm swearing. Imagine winning a stage on the Tour de France in Britain. For a British rider it's the biggest thing you can do and to have it ruined like that, not through any mistake I'd made, was really disappointing.' Cavendish admitted: 'I was crying my eyes out the last 15 miles. There's an unwritten rule that if you've crashed, or if you're behind through no fault of your own, then you get helped back to the peloton. But one commissaire stopped me doing that. It was his chance to work on the Tour and he thought his power was bigger than it was.'

What he means by this is unclear. No commissaire would have prevented him from being towed back to the bunch by a teammate, but they might have baulked at him riding behind a car, which was effectively his only option.

To rejoin a peloton travelling at around 35-40mph along Stone Street would have been physically impossible riding alone. Had his teammates waited, like McEwen's, the task would have been difficult, though

McEwen holds the stage-winner's trophy.

not impossible, but without them his only hope would have been to have sheltered in the cars' slipstreams, which is a taboo for race officials, or to cling to the side of a vehicle, which could result in disqualification.

Up at the top of the hill, Augé had, to borrow Paul Sherwen's famous expression, dug deep into his suitcase of courage to reach the 180-metre summit first and with it, he assumed, the lead of the polka-dot jersey competition.

Yet behind him a shattered Millar was being towed up the climb by his teammates and, profiting from the general lack of interest from the sprinters' teams, he stole second place on the climb and with it the jersey. It was a minor triumph for the British contingent, contrasting with the minor tragedy further down the slope, where Cavendish, still in the wooded area, was forced to switch bikes yet again, this time being handed a machine stuck in a high gear at one of the steepest parts of the course.

Augé was engulfed by the bunch within a few hundred yards of the summit, leaving the Lampre and Quickstep teams to lead the charge along Stone Street, a breathtaking, epic setting for the finale, with its views across the Stour Valley.

With 13km to go and the bunch whistling past the George Inn at Sixmile, McEwen, still off the back, was grimacing with a wrist problem.

Robbie McEwen – race winner and holder of the green jersey.

'It's a disaster for him,' Harmon said. 'This turns the whole sprinting situation on its head. Two of the favourites, young Mark Cavendish and Robbie McEwen, are effectively out of it at the moment.'

McEwen was, in fact, one of around 30 riders in a mini-bunch detached from the main field and riding so close to the cars they were committing exactly the kind of infringement Cavendish had been warned against. However, the narrowness of the road meant they had little choice. At the Chequers at Petham, with 9km to go, the McEwen group still lagged behind, but as the descent of the Chartham Downs began the road widened enough to allow the team cars to swing over, allowing the riders to bridge the gap at Fausett Hill with less than 7km to race.

Getting back on was one thing. Weaving your way through 170 riders, all riding elbow-to-elbow at well over 30mph was quite another, and one can only guess at the kind of scrapping, shoving and punching that was going on as the field went through Street End, where another huge crowd had assembled.

The Astana squad was near the front, protecting Vinokourov, though Lampre were leading the charge as the bunch entered the Nackington Road with 5km to go and homed in on Canterbury and the St Lawrence ground, the home of Kent County Cricket Club.

David Millar shakes hands with Paul Carter of KCC. Five-time Tour winner Bernard Hinault is obscured, but can be seen smiling, something he rarely did during his career.

Kelly was worried about the potential for carnage at this historic site, pointing out the acuteness of the left-hander the riders would need to take after negotiating the Nackington Road end.

It still seems incredible that 200 riders, shoe-horned into a road less than four metres wide, can simultaneously manage to tackle a 90-degree bend at that kind of speed without anyone colliding, but they all stayed upright and, having done his job, Lampre's pace-setter Alessandro Ballan peeled off the front, allowing Quickstep's Matteo Tossato to take the lead into the city.

The favourites were all now massing at the front with Boonen in third, Freire eighth or ninth and Zabel not far behind him as they entered the ring road and skirted the city's historic walls. With a single kilometre to go Milram were on the front, with Zabel poised to make his traditional fade at the line. As the sprint began he duly obliged, riding through quicksand as his rivals engulfed him and his teammates.

Barloworld's South African sprinter Robbie Hunter led the field, trailed by Discovery's Latvian rider Tom Vaitkus and the Italian Danilo Napolitano from Lampre.

At this point McEwen materialised on the left of the screen, going round the outside, and in a split second the folly of T-Mobile's decision

David Millar – King of Kent's 'mountain'.

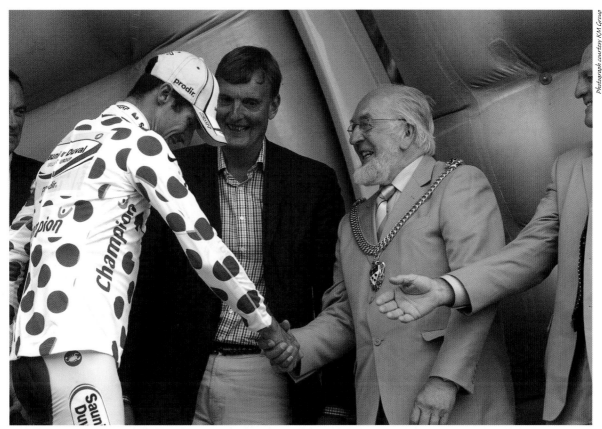

to abandon Cavendish became horrifyingly obvious. Eisel made his move with 100 metres to go, but next to McEwen he seemed to be riding in slow motion.

David Millar meets the Lord Mayor of Canterbury.

Boonen, seeing McEwen bolt past him, realised the danger and tried to latch on to his wheel, but he simply did not have the speed. With a final kick, McEwen almost mockingly crossed the line, opening up a gap on his five closest pursuers, all of whom spread themselves across the full width of the road, but whose forward progress was separated by no more than a bike length.

Boonen was pipped to second spot by a nose by the Norwegian Thor Hushovd, with two Frenchmen, Sebastien Chavanel and Romain Feillu, fourth and fifth ahead of the final member of the mini-cluster of McEwen's closest pursuers, Germany's Robert Forster. Eisel was overtaken by his teammate Marcus Berghardt, who finished eighth, in the final metres and could only finish 10th.

Zabel, to nobody's surprise, slipped back to 13th, while Hunter dropped all the way back to 21st, one place ahead of Cancellara, who comfortably retained his yellow jersey.

Of the five breakaway riders who had done so much to enliven the stage, Millar, perhaps fittingly, finished the highest in a safely anonymous

Englishman David Millar with the polka dot jersey for being king of the mountains winner

Photograph courtesy KM Group

Gusev takes the white jersey from Bernard Hinault and 'special friends'.

61st place. He moved up to third in the overall standings thanks to the time bonuses he pocketed at Gillingham and Teston.

Having admitted his ride was a 'suicide mission', Millar had at least given himself, and everyone else watching, a positive memory of the Tour's excursion to his homeland.

'The weekend has been pretty damn good, or it seems that way now,' he said. 'Today was one of those days I will never forget. It was magic. I've never seen anything like those crowds. It gave me goosebumps at times. I was very proud to be a Briton in the Tour in Britain.

'I felt I had let the side down on Saturday. Yesterday morning, I felt I hadn't done anything. I remembered that in 1994 I went to see the race [at Brighton], I waited four hours on the barriers, the break came and then Chris Boardman came and attacked the bunch and it made my day. I can still remember how excited it made me at the time, and I had that in mind today.'

He also had a tangible reward for his efforts, having snatched the polka-dot jersey from Augé on the final climb. 'The jersey and the emotions of the stage help enormously to make up for the disappointment of the prologue,' he said. 'I don't like not being in the race. My time trialling form isn't very good at the moment, but my road racing is, so I decided to use that instead. Fortunately it was one of those

Photograph courtesy KM Group

Vladimir Gusev, leader of the best young rider competition.

days when I was at my tactical best. I waited for when the first wave of attacks had slowed and then just went for it.

'It was great attacking in front of all the British crowds and I want to say a big thank you to everybody for coming out and supporting us. It was nice to hear "David, David" being called out with a British accent instead of a French one.'

Bichot was next of the attackers to cross the line, in 153rd place, with nothing to show for his efforts other than a little publicity for his team, while Grivko trailed in five places back in 158th and emerged similarly empty-handed.

Augé and Kuchynski were unable to stay with the main field. The latter trailed in over seven minutes after McEwen, the 188th and last rider to finish. Augé at least had the consolation of being awarded the prize for the day's most combative rider after he rolled in in 187th place, 2m45s behind McEwen.

'I'm a bit disappointed not to get the polka-dot jersey,' he admitted to *L'Equipe*. 'But it's no big deal, I haven't had my last word. I spent 170km on the attack and I'm starting to get used to it – I do around 3,000km per year in breakaways! I think I'm improving with age and maturing.'

Augé would go on to take the polka-dot jersey after stage three. He will also have felt a lot better than the man whose wheel he followed to the line, Cavendish, who rode with his eyes clogged by tears, to finish in 186th place. When he was later asked if he could have won, had his team opted to help him, Cavendish replied simply: 'Robbie McEwen got back…and he won.'

The following year he gave an even more emphatic answer, winning four stages in the 2008 Tour de France and announcing himself as the world's best sprinter, just as age appeared to be finally catching up with McEwen.

The Australian himself rated his victory as one of his greatest ever. 'It's incredible,' he said. 'I crashed 20km from the finish when someone hit me from behind and I went over the handlebars, landing on my hands and knees, I was hurting just about everywhere. My teammates were there and they did everything to get me back to the peloton, but I thought I didn't stand a chance in the sprint.'

Raw anger fuelled his successful pursuit. 'I found energy in rage and frustration,' he said. 'I'd really prepared well for this Tour and had the impression I'd lost everything in an instant. I told myself to stay focused and not think about my injuries. My objective was to win one stage on this Tour, so I've already succeeded.'

Victory, though a useful painkiller, could not completely blot out what had happened. 'In the heat of the moment when you get back on your bike you don't really feel anything, but now the pain is coming back, in my hand, my wrist and my knee, because when you cool down it all comes back, so I'm a bit worried about what happens next because I'm really in a bad way.'

Chapter 17

WHAT'S GOING ON?

It would be disingenuous to pretend that I knew about almost anything that had happened in the last 25km, let alone the first 100 or so, until hours, days and in some cases months afterwards.

Keeble had done another Lewis Hamilton impression to get us to the line 20 minutes before the riders arrived, and, his work for the day done, he was trying to work out how he could avoid giving Gilles a lift back to Larkfield.

Hobson and I, however, were discovering just how impersonal the Tour de France could be, even for supposedly accredited media. Our laminated plastic passes were enough to get us through the first set of protective barriers, but, despite assurances that we would get access to the riders, no further.

During 2007, the average attendance at events I covered was around 500 and I was usually the only reporter. In Canterbury alone there were over three times as many journalists as there were supporters at the previous football game I had covered, Walton Casuals versus Maidstone United, back in April.

There was no repeat of the Tour of Britain scoop from 2006, when we were ushered into the top trailer (an oxymoronic concept perhaps) and treated to Kristian House's stream of conciousness. Instead we found a vacant spot by a roadside barrier, with a view of the big screen, and saw about three seconds of live action, during which it was impossible to make out which rider was which due to the speed at which they entered and exited our field of vision.

It was obvious that McEwen had won as the deafening public address system was bellowing his name out in a heavy French accent, but how we would get hold of him, Millar, or anyone else who had actually ridden the stage was less apparent.

The calculation was easy enough. There were eight hacks for every rider and as almost everyone wanted to talk to the same half-dozen people there was no way we could all congregate in the podium area. We watched the presentations and were then told the media centre was a quarter of a mile away at the Canterbury High School in Knight Avenue. The school's gym doubled as the press area and after the euphoria of riding in the race car it was a faintly deflating experience to step inside the hall and realise you were just one of 1,500 jobbing journos, most of whom were hunched over their laptops waiting for the official results to arrive.

The riders did not even come to the hall – instead you submitted written questions via a press officer and took pot luck that they would submit them to the selected riders, who were back at the finish line and spoke to the hall via a live video link. There was little point in feeling put out by it, although I could not help but wish I had been a bit more French about the whole thing and demanded our agreements be honoured.

In reality it probably made no difference. To grab a scoop on the Tour you either need to be incredibly lucky, as I was with House a year earlier, or to have built up a relationship with a rider, like Fotheringham had with Millar. Riders like Wiggins were contracted to newspapers and cycling magazines and were therefore never going to tell you anything they would not tell a hundred other people, while the polyglot McEwen was in demand with the French and Dutch-speaking hacks as well as the anglophones.

McEwen sat on a sofa a few hundred metres away and we dutifully noted down his utterances, followed by those of Cancellara, so that we could at least say we got these first-hand.

Fabian Cancellara retained the yellow jersey, and met the Lord Mayor of Canterbury.

Photograph courtesy KM Group

Fabian Cancellara on the podium.

Half an hour later and, for us, the Tour was over. The majority of the 1,500 packed up and made their way down the A2 to Dover for the ferry to the next stage. Hobson headed to Canterbury East, attempting to find a train that could get him back to his home in Lewisham, and I lugged my laptop to my brother's house in Roper Road, passing the Bernards, Hinault and Thevenet, on the way, both of them dressed in the blue blazers and cream trousers that formed the unofficial uniform of Tour employees and which made them look almost like a couple of well-tanned cricket duffers.

Chapter 18

'ACT LIKE THE ENGLISH'

The riders' experiences of the stage contrasted drastically, but what everyone agreed on was the quality of the course and the turn-out. Cancellara's post-stage tribute was typical: 'The crowd was incredible, I've never seen that on the Tour de France before. I have a message for the French – they should act like the English and turn out in numbers on the roadside to encourage us.'

Tour Director Christian Prudhomme echoed Cancellara, saying: 'The enormous crowds in Kent have taken our breath away. The Tour has been staggered by the warm reception we have been given by the British public.'

The French media waxed lyrical – a little too lyrical in some cases. If any of them were struggling to avoid cliché and stereotype, they failed spectacularly.

'The peace and tranquility of the magnificent Kent countryside did not anaesthetise this first stage, ridden, rhythmically, from London and its Tower Bridge to Canterbury and its cathedral, a famous venue for numerous French students on excursions,' *L'Equipe* purred, using the kind of language you can only get away with in French.

The stage was a lot harder than some of the foreign journalists had expected.

Guillaume Prébois, like Geoff Thomas, was riding the entire route, in his case 24 hours ahead of the peloton, and he wrote of 'permanent ascents and descents, head winds and traffic jams' in *Le Monde*: 'It's a really tough start. Frankly we did not have the time to take English tea during the first stage. It was the equivalent of going up Alpe d'Huez!'

Elsewhere in *Le Monde*, Marc Roche went even further. His colour piece was headlined: 'Kent salutes with fervour a Tour absent from Her Majesty's screens', in a reference to the lack of terrestrial television coverage for the stage. The author used a mildly worrying analogy that compared the English crowds to a public schoolgirl, who, given a sniff of

Fabian Cancellara pulls on the yellow jersey.

freedom after years of being brought up in a strict school, turns into some kind of nymphomaniac. 'Once you undo the lace, the girl explodes,' Roche wrote. 'And this is what happened on 8 July, in stuck-up Canterbury, seat of the Church of England.'

Anthony Masters from KmFm was quoted in the French daily, saying: 'The whole of Kent has descended onto the streets. It was simply colossal.'

In any other circumstances that would have sounded a little over the top but, given the context of the article, Masters was being relatively restrained.

The left-wing daily *Libération* ran a slightly baffling colour piece that once again suggested its author, Jean-Louis Le Touzet, had rifled through a dictionary of English stereotypes before firing up his laptop. Translating it into English proved difficult because if you attempted to do it literally you were left with something fit only for Pseuds' Corner in *Private Eye*.

'The Tour has now left the land of Dickens, the Archbishop of Canterbury and minted mutton, where it was an immense popular success. Yesterday, the 203km stage unfurled in Kent, where we could admire these English people, who don't just get themselves excited for the jockey club. The English, just like the French, cherish these great summer migrations on the roadside. It was excellent news for the Tour, which, like the Vatican, displayed a cardinal pomp in its new mission territory.'

In French it sounded like drivel, for a simple reason. It was drivel.

On this side of the Channel *The Daily Mail*, not usually guilty of underselling things, could not quite reach the heights of pretension touched by *Libération*, but Ivan Speck managed a suitably bombastic introduction for the paper's notoriously patriotic readers. 'Even Chaucer would not have scripted a *Millar's Tale* as uplifting as the one which ended in Canterbury with a polka-dot jersey for Britain's finest,' he wrote, presumably while listening to *Jerusalem* on his iPod. 'From the depths of a two-year ban for doping, David Millar scrambled his way back to the front of the cycling world yesterday. He may not have been the first man to finish stage one of the 2007 Tour de France, but for an hour through the Medway towns of Kent, the Scot repaid a debt of thanks to a public who have never given up on him.'

The red-top tabloids did little more than regurgitate press releases – both *The Sun* and *The Mirror* parrotted a claim that four million people had been watching on the Sunday, a figure that in fact included the estimate given for the London prologue, but the broadsheets were more at home with cycling.

The Times ran an article headlined 'Pilgrims Flock to Canterbury', co-authored by Owen Slot and David Sanderson, about the way the success of the stage confounded the expectations of a section of the French media.

'Road cycling in Britain is like an enormous secret society, but the Tour seemed to send out a clarion call to all. At the stroke of midnight on Saturday, four young Yorkshiremen, Jamie Sindall, Jake Barker, Isaac Cameron and Charlie Muff, left home in Leeds and drove south.'

It sounded like the authors were straying into Monty Python territory.

'The four 18-year-olds arrived in the village of Goudhurst at 5am, half an hour before trucks arrived with the fencing and advertising hoardings. Once there, the quartet were able to stake their claim to the best spot, atop a hill where nine hours later the village would build a fanatical wave of applause as the riders wormed their way towards them. Back in Leeds, their mates thought they were plain mad, but as Goudhurst came to life yesterday morning, the four friends found themselves in the company of like-minded souls.'

In *The Guardian* a couple of days later, Fotheringham offered one of the clearest explanations of the stage's success. 'The Tour is invited abroad because it brings special things with it, less tangible but arguably more important things than the many millions of pounds in revenue for hotels, restaurants and bars that Ken Livingstone kept hammering on about.

'To start with, the Tour is an excuse for a big day out, which is strange given that most people in Kent actually saw the cyclists for roughly a minute as they whizzed past. It is about far more than merely standing by the roadside watching a cycle race.'

It is. Sadly, this unquestionable triumph was about to be given a fresh perspective.

EPILOGUE

It would probably depress Noel Coward to know that of all the contributions he made to English culture, I remember him best for his final role, that of the underworld gangster Mr Bridger in the seminal film *The Italian Job*.

The Man of Kent may have written *Brief Encounter*, *Mad Dogs and Englishmen*, *The Vortex*, *A Room With a View* and been knighted into the bargain, but for me he will always be the boiler-suited old lag who funded Michael Caine's Turin heist. Coward only appeared in the film because his adopted son, Peter Collinson, was the director, but with the obvious exception of Caine's lament about only blowing the bloody doors off, he was given the majority of the film's best lines.

These included a dialogue with the actor Tony Beckley, who played Coward's maître d', Camp Freddie. The two men are discussing whether Benny Hill's character can be persuaded to join their nefarious scheme, when a panicked Beckley asks, 'But what if he isn't bent?'

To which Coward replies witheringly 'Camp Freddie, everyone in the world is bent.'

By the third week of July 2007, I was beginning to think Coward had a point.

The Tour de France, which had swept through Kent on a wave of euphoria just two weeks beforehand, was imploding. The race was churning out scandals at a rate that made its imminent death seem inevitable. I had reached the point where I no longer wanted to care, but still did.

As part of the *Kent Messenger*'s deal with ASO, we were obliged to cover the race for its entire duration, which meant updating the *kentonline* website after every stage. In practice this also meant updating the site every time a doping story broke and it became a singularly depressing experience.

I knew this represented a high watermark in my career. After this, it was going to be difficult to go back to rewriting reports about seven-a-side rugby tournaments in Cranbrook and angling off the coast of Sheppey, but I thought the euphoria might keep me going for a little while longer than the fortnight it took for it to evaporate completely.

The first week of the race passed largely without incident, but the first whiff of trouble came on 18 July, when Patrik Sinkewitz, a 26-year-old

German who had already crashed out of the race with a broken nose, was revealed to have tested 'non-negative' for testosterone during a pre-race training camp.

This was not good news, but Sinkewitz was a non entity, a T-Mobile domestique who would have struggled to win the race on a Harley.

A week later, however, and the story I dreaded writing most of all broke. Vinokourov had tested positive for 'homologous blood doping' after winning the stage 13 time trial in Albi. By that point injuries he had sustained from crashing meant he was all but out of contention for the yellow jersey, but there had been something heroic about the way he eclipsed the time trial specialists to take the stage. He had a disastrous 14th stage, but recovered the following day with an apparently epic display in the Pyrenees, attacking on the Col de Peyresourde to win in Le Louron.

This simply proved Fotheringham's adage: if a performance looks too good to be true, then it probably is.

David Millar, who idolised Vinokourov, was distraught when told the news. 'Jesus Christ – there you go, that's my quote,' he said. 'What timing, huh? This is just f****** great.' In a remark directed at Paul Kimmage, Millar implied the Irish writer had got what he wanted: 'Well there you go, Paul.'

This was perhaps unfair on Kimmage, who always said he'd rather be covering golf than exposing yet another drug scandal, but in the heat of the moment Millar seemed to be on the point of giving up on the sport.

'I wanted to believe it was a really good day. It makes me very sad. Vino is one of my favourite riders. He's one of the most beautiful riders in the peloton. If a guy of his stature and class has done that, we all might as well pack our bags and go home right now.' But then, after reflecting for a while, he had a change of heart. 'The Tour de France should go on. If it stops, I would have to retire tomorrow. The irony here is that I was hoping to make an announcement today about my future plans, I have some projects in the works. I am hoping to work with young riders, to show them that you don't have to dope to succeed.'

The fact that he subsequently broke down in tears suggested these hopes were in tatters. Vinokourov inevitably protested his innocence, claiming the results could be explained by the large amount of blood he had in his thigh after the stage.

He even managed a joke. 'I heard that I made a transfusion with my father's blood,' Vinokourov said. 'That's absurd, I can tell you that with his blood, I would have tested positive for vodka.'

What followed proved Victor Meldrew's rule: just when you think things can't get any worse – they get worse.

On 25 July the race leader, Michael Rasmussen, scored an apparently decisive victory in the race's final mountain stage over his only serious rival, Alberto Contador. But within hours the 33-year-old Dane was withdrawn from the race by his Rabobank team. Six days earlier Rasmussen had been dropped from the Danish national team after failing to tell the truth about his whereabouts in the build-up to the race.

For British sports fans the case would have uncomfortable parallels with the story of the 400-metre gold medal-winning athlete Christine Ohuruogu. Like Ohuruogu, Rasmussen never failed a drug test, but on three occasions in the build-up to the Tour he failed to inform dope testers of his precise location.

Unlike Ohuruogu, who was generally believed when she claimed to be guilty of nothing more sinister than absent-mindedness, Rasmussen was unable to offer a plausible explanation for his missed tests. The pressure on the Dane grew, but he appeared to thrive on it, putting in a series of decisive performances and playing the wounded victim role to perfection in post-race interviews. All the while the public jeered as his story unravelled.

He made convincing pleas of innocence at a specially arranged press conference designed to kill the story, but fatally claimed his elusiveness was due to the fact he had been training in Mexico. He had, in fact, been training in the Dolomites, though but for a chance encounter there with the Italian race analyst Davide Cassani, his duplicity might have gone undetected.

Rasmussen had not tested positive for any banned substance, but his credibility was in tatters. His team manager, Theo de Rooy, sent him home, handing Contador a yellow jersey that no longer seemed worth winning.

Contador would win this least coveted of Tours the following Sunday in Paris, but by then there was further collateral damage. Cristian Moreni, a 34-year-old Italian whose career was every bit as nondescript as Sinkewitz's, had tested positive for testosterone. He was arrested by police in Pau and, with a spectator screaming 'Con!' (a French expletive that needs little translation) at him, was bundled into a van, along with the entire Cofidis team – including Bradley Wiggins, who was treated like a criminal, even though he was one of the race's obvious victims.

On stage six Wiggins had attacked just 2km after the start and stayed away until 7km from the finish. Riding against a clean peloton he might never have been caught.

Cofidis abandoned the Tour and Wiggins contemplated giving up the sport.

This was the Tour's darkest hour since 1998, but there were, for the terminal optimists, signs that this time the dopers had lost the one thing that allowed them to continue – the indulgence of their fellow riders and the public.

At the start of stage 16 a riders' protest had been organised. Past demonstrations were usually indignant cyclists protesting about the heavy-handedness of the police, who failed to accord them the dignity many of them manifestly didn't deserve.

This time, however, a number of riders, predominantly French, were protesting against drug cheats, at last suggesting a willingness to tackle the conspiracy of silence that had been complicit in allowing the cheats to prosper.

Wiggins had opted not to join the protest, but in a chilling yet brilliant column he wrote for *The Observer* on the Sunday the 2007 race finished, he revealed the precise moment he realised he had been duped.

'I decided not to wait on the line because I don't want to be dictated to,' he wrote. 'People know where I stand. I was in 100 per cent agreement with them, but I have friends in other teams who aren't French and are clean. I didn't want to watch them ride off and be saying, in effect, that they were on drugs because they weren't with us.'

Wiggins set off after the peloton and caught them, only to make an appalling realisation.

'When I caught up, everyone was laughing, patting me on the back and saying well done for coming with us,' he said. 'I heard some awful things at that point, which made me very depressed – the worst was one rider who joked that he didn't understand the French, that if they took drugs they would go faster and why didn't they try it?'

Despite his initial dejection, Wiggins still managed to offer genuine hope for the future. 'I don't see why guys like me should suffer because of a minority,' he wrote. 'There are riders like Geraint Thomas, who are the future, riders like the ones at Française des Jeux who are coming through, and there are guys like David Millar, who is a real ambassador for anti-doping. Things will get better. The people who are still doping are mainly the older generation and the riders who hang around with them. The sooner they are gone the better.'

There was no point in denying that lasting damage had been done to the sport. More than one person told me they felt everything they had seen on 8 July had been a sham, an opinion reflected in a *Kent Messenger* editorial entitled simply: 'We Were Conned'.

For the first four days after the Kent stage I was consumed with trying to make sense of around 2,000 pictures taken by our photographers and submitted by readers, then cramming them into a 24-page special supplement, writing articles and also trying to produce our usual sports section.

Thereafter it was difficult to escape this clawing sense of negativity, but to make the knee-jerk claim that the events of 8 July should be flung on history's compost heap was simplistic and naive.

For a start it was a tremendous insult to the likes of Millar, Augé and McEwen, who had produced such a superb stage. And more fundamentally, it asked us to believe that the Tour de France ought to exist in a utopia, cocooned from the dark forces that affect every other aspect of society.

The Tour de France cannot be isolated from life itself. The pressures that tempt and compel cyclists to gain an unfair advantage at the expense of their rivals are the same as the pressures that lead people to bend and break laws in every sport that has ever been played, or, to broaden the point, sell vulnerable people sub-prime mortgages.

If we define a great player as an individual who makes a greater contribution to his team's success than any other, the two greatest team sportsmen of the 20th century were Diego Maradona and Shane Warne, both of whom may have been elevated to the status of gods by excitable sports writers and awe-struck fans, but both of whom succumbed to human temptations, including apparently performance-enhancing substances.

Cheating in football and cricket takes many forms, from diving to win a penalty, to appealing for a catch when a fielder knows a batsman hasn't hit the ball. Part of cycling's problem is that the most effective way to cheat is to take drugs, and the very word is so emotive that reason usually flies out of the window as soon as it mentioned.

Whatever Rasmussen did during the time he spent AWOL, it is unlikely that it had as decisive an effect as Maradona palming the ball into Peter Shilton's net in the 1986 World Cup.

Wiggins also pointed out something that had largely been forgotten in the rush to condemn the dopers. Most of them were actually nice guys who, like Millar, had cracked under pressure. Vinokourov was a gentleman. Moreni had a playful sense of humour and called him 'Lord Wiggins'.

Wiggins thought they were 'bastards' for what they had done, but his column showed it was possible to hate the crimes someone had committed while simultaneously feeling human sympathy for them.

Recognising we are all flawed beings does not mean we should allow people to get away with cheating, drug-taking and racketeering, but nor should the Tour's failings blind us to its greatness. It is, and will remain, a magnificent event.

In a piece written before the scandals broke, Fotheringham attempted to explain. 'As the scenes in central London's parks showed, the Tour is as much an outdoor festival as a cycle race, and as Kent's villages found out, it can bring communities together as they organise the stuff that makes the Tour's coming special: fêtes, bands, barbecues, booze, posters, flags.

'Any one-off major sports event brings those things with it, but the Tour has one unique difference compared to, say, the World Cup or an Olympic Games. It actually comes to places like Goudhurst and Bethersden, and to tiny hamlets in lost parts of rural France. The involvement is absolute, total and direct.'

If anyone doubts this, they need only to look at some of the superb pictures in this book and the expressions on the faces of some of the fans who watched from Kent's roadsides on 8 July.

Better still, dig out a copy of the Eurosport and ITV4 coverage of the event. If you're a Kent native it's difficult to suppress the thrill you'll feel from watching the riders tackle roads you've ridden on and driven along a thousand times.

Watch David Millar's personal journey towards redemption through Gravesend, Rochester, Maidstone and Tunbridge Wells, see how devastated Mark Cavendish was at crashing and marvel at how Robbie McEwen managed to thread his way back through the peloton to stun the likes of Tom Boonen.

The biggest thrill of all is watching an entire county mobilised for such a uniquely positive, energising event.

8 July 2007 was the greatest day of my professional life. I had a race-side seat at the Tour de France, I mingled with cyclists I had idolised while growing up and I was able to experience what it felt like to drive along roads lined with two million people, all of whom had turned out to watch the world's greatest annual sporting event, here in Kent.

Vive le Tour.

LEGACY

At the time of writing, 18 months after the event, the legacy of the Tour's trip to Kent is difficult to measure. The first consideration is purely practical. Is it actually any safer to ride a bike in Kent?

Based on anecdotal evidence alone, the answer has to be no. Traffic on the roads has, if anything, increased, but this has not been matched by a discernible improvement in cycle lanes.

In the county town a journey across the centre by bike is far more dangerous than using either a car or a bus. To cross the River Medway, for example, the only safe and legal option is to use the cycle lane on the new bridge. Cyclists are not legally allowed to use either the High Level Bridge or the Millennium Bridge, adding needless extra minutes to every journey.

In reality these regulations are ignored. Prosecutions for cycling on pavements are unheard of and which parent would tell their child to compete with four lanes of traffic on the road bridges when they could use a pedestrian alternative?

By the same logic, someone riding into town on the Tonbridge Road has to deal with the full wrath of the one-way system. It might not be legal to use the pavement, but if a cyclist hits a pedestrian at 10mph, he or she will do a lot less damage than a motorist would hitting a cyclist at more than 30mph.

Where cycle lanes exist they are often treated as additional parking bays by motorists, because parking in a cycle lane is ignored by traffic wardens.

From a sporting point of view, the race stimulated interest to an extent. Clubs reported an increase in membership and participation in racing has increased, albeit not to the extent that it could be considered a majority sport. Time trialling and road racing has seen a 50 per cent increase, but there are unlikely to be more than 150 riders in any one event – you would find more participants in certain darts leagues.

Then there is the economy. Kent Cycles reported a brief surge of business after the Tour, one that was replicated after Great Britain's success in the velodrome in Beijing a year later.

The effect was short-term, however.

Matt Davison estimates it gave Kent's economy a short-term cash injection, but is sceptical about any durable impact. 'A lot of people around the world would have seen that Kent is a really beautiful place and I think the TV coverage did us a lot of favours,' he said. 'I certainly think that people didn't mind public money being spent on it, because a lot of people will have seen it and decided to visit Kent, but I don't think personally that it had much of an effect in the longer term.'

Graham Baldwin, however, suggests a certain amount of business has been drummed up by people retracing the Tour's route.

'At Tenterden station we'll quite often get cyclists here in the summer who aren't here for the steam trains but are stopping for refreshment because they are riding the route.'

Caution should be exercised by anyone wishing to do this in its entirety.

In fact it is not legally possible to ride the entire stage route now, nor would it be sensible to attempt it, even if cyclists were allowed through the Medway tunnel. The first section inside the M25 is just too dangerous and the scenery doesn't justify an excursion. Things improve after Gravesend, but the first section really suitable for cycling is along the Pilgrim's Way between Rochester and Kit's Coty. Maidstone, Tonbridge, Tunbridge Wells and Ashford are all great bases for bike rides into the surrounding countryside, but their centres should all be avoided. If anyone is looking to recreate a part of the stage, their best bet would be the stretch between Capel and Tenterden, or the final leg from Sellindge to Canterbury, where you may just find a fellow lycra-clad enthusiast following in David Millar's footsteps.

The most durable legacy, however, is perhaps in people's memories.

The San Fairy Ann club continue to ride through the Weald, with Martyn Peal acting as a Tour guide.

Even now Peal says he gets a tingle down his spine every time he thinks about the race passing through his village. When he visits the local farm shop, his five-year-old son, strapped to the back of his tandem, asks if they can sprint for David Millar's sign, and on club runs Peal always makes a point of saying 'The Tour came through here' to any uninitiated members of the group.

Everyone I interviewed for this book was able to look back on 8 July 2007 with an overwhelming feeling of fondness, and some went as far as to say it was the greatest day of their lives.

It is difficult to think of any single event that has had a comparable effect on the county's psyche.

The 1987 hurricane may have touched similar numbers of people, but that was a tale of survival, acts of God and awe at the power of nature.

When the people of Kent look back at the Tour de France, most will smile, and if this book rekindles just some of those memories of that day, it will have been worthwhile.

FURTHER READING

The 2007 Tour generated thousands of articles, some of which were written by people who actually knew what they were talking about.

The Guardian's William Fotheringham is a beacon of sanity and his book *Roule Britannia* is as close to essential as a cycling book can be.

For a general overview of the race, try Tim Moore's *French Revolutions*, *Le Tour* by Geoffrey Wheatcroft, or *Tour de France: The Official Centennial*, by *L'Equipe*, Lance Armstrong and Jean-Marie Leblanc.

Paul Kimmage produced one of the best books ever written about cycling, *A Rough Ride*, his memoir of a desperate career as a clean professional rider trying to compete against dopers. His articles for *The Sunday Times* on the 2007 Tour are among the best examples of sports journalism and can still be found at *www.timesonline.co.uk*.

Matt Rendell's biography *The Death of Marco Pantani* is similarly compelling, but, as the title suggests, there is no happy ending and it is not an uplifting read.

Bradley Wiggins's column at the end of the 2007 Tour is also worth reading again in full at *www.guardian.co.uk*.

For an insight into the mindset of a cyclist, try Tim Krabbe's novel *The Rider*.

The *Kent Messenger* produced supplements before and after the race, both of which are available to view at the newspaper's HQ in Larkfield and local libraries.

The author also wrote a Tour diary for *www.kentonline.co.uk* in the build-up to the race, which remains online.

ACKNOWLEDGEMENTS

This book could not have been written without the help of the following people. Ron Green and Barry Hollis of the *Kent Messenger* generously allowed me to use their pictures, without which this project would never have got off the ground.

The two photographers who rode shotgun on the day were Barry Goodwin and Jamie Gray, both of whom did something I wasn't prepared to do, namely put my life in the hands of a motorcycle driver.

Ron Keeble made 8 July 2007 an unforgettable experience for me in more ways than one. Paul Hobson and Toby Gilles kept me company in Ron's car and a number of the *KM*'s other photographers and reporters took pictures from the roadside, including Matthew Walker, Andy Payton, Barry Hollis, Jim Rantell, Grant Falvey, Barry Crayford, Gary Browne, Sam Lennon, Phil Houghton, John Westhrop, David Antony Hunt, Jason Dodd, Trisha Fermor, Matthew Reading and Chris Hunter.

Amanda Lumley from Kent County Council and Delphine Houlton from Maxim were also extremely generous with time and advice, the former also providing number of excellent photos taken by KCC's team.

The following provided stories, advice and encouragement: Gary Chalkley and Dave Mackey of Kent Cycles; The San Fairy Ann Cycling Club, particularly Ron Lee, Patsy Hill, Keir Williams and Clive Bradburn; The Ashford Wheelers, particularly David Roe and Graham Galpin; Medway Velo Club's Phil Callow and Rob Kennison.

A number of people very kindly submitted pictures, including Tunbridge Wells Borough Council, Stuart Phillips, David Hodgkinson, Diane Fryd, Hilary Yorke, Alan Constable, John Kavanagh, Jamie Webb, Mike Flynn, Gary King, Ian Williams, Clive Bradburn and Colin Flockton.